Exercises in Criticism

"Louis Bury's provocative and pleasurably disarming constraint-based pursuit of a critical engagement with contemporary constraint-based writing, as well as with the nature of criticism itself, makes for a lively, searching investigation — a kind of practice-based reportage from the outskirts of literary sense. In one sense *Exercises in Critisim* is a useful and quite particular survey/demonstration of Oulipo-influenced methodologies enacted by a range of North American experimental writers in the last half-century. At the same time Bury builds into the book an imaginative and surprisingly intimate use of transcription that allows him to handle constraint and certain types of self-imposed pressure as simultaneous partners and foils. The result is an engrossing, lived-in and distinctly available read that examines pre-selected limits while redefining and pushing past its own."

— Anselm Berrigan

"The creative criticism — or critical creativity — on display in Louis Bury's *Exercises in Criticism* seems to me exactly what's needed — or, for this reader anyway, most desirable — in literary inquiry today. Bury's 'foregrounding [of] academic work as an indirect means of self-exploration' manages to expand both the self at stake and its many objects of obsession. Amidst all its clever experimentation, Bury's book also offers real and deep thoughts about the legacy of the Oulipo, relations between capitalism and academia, the source and sustenance of intellectual investments throughout a life, and the web made by familial and political history. I laud its thoroughness, its play, its risks, its transmutation of dissatisfactions into art."

— Maggie Nelson

"Welcome to the brilliantly high-risk cabinet of Louis Bury — prestidigitator, virtuoso, ethicist, scholar, gambler, mimic, poet. In and out of chains, this Houdini is a master of escape tactics. *Exercises in Criticism* is at once an encyclopedia of Oulipian procedures, and a utopian Grand Grimoire, showing how to practice literary criticism as a lifesaving, joy-bringing regime. Cool codes dominate this manual, but its secret core is soulful, intimate, and emotionally urgent."

— Wayne Koestenbaum

Copyright ©2014 by Louis Bury. First edition, 2014. All rights reserved

Excerpts from previous versions of this book first appeared, often in different forms, in the following publications: *Anamesa*, *Drunken Boat*, *Electronic Book Review*, EOAGH, *Jacket Magazine*, *Lies/Isle*, *Modern Language Studies*, *Shampoo*, *Transverse*, and *The Volta*. Many thanks to their editors.

Library of Congress Cataloging-in-Publication Data
Exercises in criticism : the theory and practice of literary constraint / Louis Bury. -- First edition.
   pages cm
ISBN 978-1-62897-105-7 (pbk. : alk. paper)
1. Literature, Modern--History and criticism. I. Title.
PN710.B87 2015
809'.04--dc23
            2014031524

 Partially funded by a grant from the Illinois Arts Council, a state agency.

The author would like to thank the NYU Humanities Initiative, as well as G. Gabrielle Starr, Seryl Kushner Dean, College of Arts and Sciences, and Pat C. Hoy II, former Director of the Expository Writing Program, for their vital funding support for this publication.

As part of its methodology, this book occasionally samples or appropriates language without the use of quotation marks. Most such borrowings are acknowledged through explanatory framing devices; some are not. In all instances, these borrowings are deployed for artistic and methodological effect.

www.dalkeyarchive.com

Cover: design and composition by Mikhail Iliatov
Printed on permanent/durable acid-free paper

Louis Bury

Exercises in Criticism:
The Theory and Practice
of Literary Constraint

DALKEY ARCHIVE PRESS
Champaign / London / Dublin

Contents

Exiting the Labyrinth 3

Preamble 9

Prospectus 11
Introduction 21

Anticipatory Plagiary 37

Raymond Roussel's (New) Africa 39
Reading *I Remember* (on Joe Brainard) 47

Oulipo 55

The Exercise and Oulipo (on Raymond Queneau) 57
The N+7 Form 73
Masturbation: A Manifesto (on Harry Mathews) 77

Post-Oulipo 87

Bernadette Mayer's Gratuitous Art 89
Errata 5uite: 20 Questions (on Joan Retallack) 95
Gold Fools and the Question of Narrative (on Gilbert Sorrentino) 101
Ideas for an Essay on *the tapeworm foundry*
(on Darren Wershler-Henry) 107
Cunt-ups: An Exegesis (on Dodie Bellamy) 111
The Cunning Linguist (on Harryette Mullen) 117
Absences, Negations, Voids (on Doug Nufer) 121
Job Talk (on Doug Nufer) 129
Cultural Politics, Postmodernism, and White Guys:
Femininity as Affect and Effect in Robert Fitterman's *This Window Makes Me Feel* 133
Dies, a Sentence (on Vanessa Place) 143
Not-Reading Kenneth Goldsmith 147
Love Letter to CAConrad 157
Interview with Ammiel Alcalay 163

Contents

The Clinamen 183

Notebook Excerpts 185
An Oulipolooza: *from* the Q&A (on poker and constraint) 201
One should not try to go over the limit (on my father) 205
To the fact, to the point, to the bottom line (on my grandmother) 217
Therapy 293
The Defense 309

Bibliography 329

Acknowledgments 333

Exercises in Critisism

Exiting the Labyrinth

> Oulipians: rats who construct the labyrinth
> from which they propose to escape.
> —Raymond Queneau

After years inside this literary labyrinth, I at last see, squintingly, its exit. My eyes, I can tell, will have trouble adjusting to the naked light of day. During my time here, as I designed ever more elaborate involutions, I wasn't particularly concerned with finding my way out: inside, the potential intricacies were endless, consuming. Even now, as I exit so that you can enter, the way out I've discovered resembles nothing so much as the way I got in: more reading, more writing, more note taking—the evolving blueprint for a new labyrinth to construct and explore.

In colloquial English, "labyrinth" and "maze" are used more or less interchangeably but, strictly speaking, a maze refers to a complex branching puzzle with choices of path and direction while a labyrinth has only a single, non-branching path that leads to its center. Escape from a labyrinth, therefore, *pace* Queneau, is mostly a formality: unlike with a maze, safe passage in and out is never in any real doubt. To conceive of exiting as an escape implies that the labyrinth's author doesn't want to be stuck inside, is in fact stuck. But when entrapment is voluntarily elected, again and again, it hardly can be called entrapment. Writers, constrained or otherwise, only escape works-in-progress in the sense that lobsters can be said to escape their shells, trading in the old carapace for a newer, perhaps different-fitting one.

The comparison to shells is more than mere analogy: books, especially labyrinthine ones, are carapaces, fortresses, vaults. We inhabit them, readers and writers alike, as temporary strongholds. No matter their structural integrity is precarious: with thick walls of words textual labyrinths attempt to entomb, at center—like Daedalus penning in the Minotaur—unwelcome presences, psychic nuisances, monstrosities. But a labyrinth, no matter how elaborate, does not make for an airtight tomb; a repressed presence cannot remain absent forever. Both await—half-forgotten, mysterious—some questing Theseus, string and sword in hand, to confront the buried beast.

As you retrace my footsteps through these mirrored corridors, in search of the knowledge mummified within, understand that whatever living creatures once dwelt here have long since disappeared, become ghosts. What glimpses of them you catch are but reflections in a mirror, reflections of reflections, faint shadows of shades in a literary funhouse. Understand, too, that it took me so long to depart, even after most of my work here was done, because, like other backward souls, I feel more lost outside a labyrinth than in one.

Louis Bury
New York City
July 2013

The moment a limit is posited it is overstepped, and that against which the limit was established is absorbed.
—Theodor Adorno, *Minima Moralia*

To be in any form, what is that?
—Walt Whitman

Preamble

Prospectus

: Context

I include this prospectus at the outset both because it introduces the book's conceit better, more succinctly, than the "Introduction" that follows it and also because, having herein outlined the book's proposed turns of argument, I thereafter felt liberated from the dry task of having to expound them.

: What was I trying to do?

Looking back, it's apparent, and amusing, just how many of the prospectus' ostensibly intellectual concerns were first and foremost personal ones. When, for example, I diagnosed the work of Christian Bök and Harryette Mullen as representative constrained responses to a "widespread loneliness" in American culture, I was also trying to account for, even justify, my own feelings of "loneliness, depression and boredom" at the time. "All dissertations," contends poet Ammiel Alcalay, "are very personal things," "no matter how dry and scholarly [they may appear]." Eventually I stopped trying to pretend otherwise.

Prospectus

Abstract
This book will be an exercise in applied poetics, using constraint-based methods in order to write about literary constraint. I define literary constraint as literature that imposes rules and restrictions upon itself over and above the rules and restrictions (such as grammar and lexicon) inherent in language—as literature that understands itself as part of an avant-garde tradition whose most prominent precursor is the work of Oulipo, or "Workshop For Potential Literature," a French writing group, founded in 1960 and still active today, whose purpose is to invent arbitrary constraints for the purposes of generating literary texts. When complete, the book will contain ninety-nine short chapters, each of which follows a different compositional procedure. By tracing the lineage and enduring influence of early Oulipian classics, I argue that contemporary English-language writers have, in their adoption of constraint-based methods, transformed such methods from apolitical literary laboratory exercises into a form of cultural critique whose usage is surprisingly widespread in contemporary literature, particularly among poets and experimental novelists.

Methodological Rationale
In the fifty-year history of Oulipo, its members have contrived innumerable constraints for the purposes of generating literary texts, from Georges Perec's famous lipogrammatic novel *La Disparition* (written without using any word containing the letter e) to techniques that have attained cult status in avant-garde circles, like the N+7 technique (in which every noun in a source text is replaced by the seventh one following it in the dictionary), as well as more obscure techniques like Mathews' Algorithm (an elaborate permutational procedure). Yet despite the group's prolific and varied output, none of its members have more than dabbled with constraint for the purposes of generating critical work. Given that Oulipian techniques have been transposed, fruitfully, to realms of endeavor as diverse as cooking, comic book art, and musical composition, it is surprising that something similar has never been systematically attempted in the critical realm.

The practice of criticism, literary or otherwise, always imposes rules and restrictions upon its practitioners, though they are not usually thought of as such. At the most basic level, criticism has an obligation to be useful, to explicate or illuminate the texts of others. Further, different critical practices and contexts carry with them different goals and imperatives: book reviews place different demands upon critics than scholarly monographs; the differing philosophical or ideological assumptions that underlie critical schools typically lead to widely differing conceptions of the critic's required task. And, too, there are myriad tacit or openly enforced stylistic and argumentative conventions of criticism: citational systems; standards of logical reasoning and acceptable evidence; an objective, authoritative tone; etc. The extent to which each of these rules, assumptions, and criteria can be properly said to be constraints of the kind Oulipo concocts matters less, in this context, than that they are pervasive in critical discourse, and, in important ways, determinative of that discourse's content and shape.

The standards and conventions of contemporary literary criticism exist for good reason but are too often regarded as immutable, almost — ironic, given critical theory's penchant for debunking myths of normativity — natural. Through the sometimes arbitrary imposition of rules and restrictions upon itself my book asks what happens to the critical act when its conditions are altered? For example, what would happen were critics confined to raising questions without being allowed to answer them? My interrogative chapter on Gilbert Sorrentino's interrogative novel, *Gold Fools*, addresses this question through both its form and its content. And though the decision to confine myself to the use of interrogatives precludes the possibility of definitively answering the question, it becomes apparent, through such an exercise, just how suggestively generative the mere act of posing questions is to criticism, even when answers are not forthcoming. In this way, in addition to being an exegesis of various constraint-based texts, my book is also an investigation into the nature of criticism itself: its form, its function, its utility, its ethical imperatives — its limits.

By imposing unusual forms upon my critical prose, I seek to kindle what Harry Mathews, one of two American members of Oulipo, identifies as constraint's inherent value: "being unable to say what you normally would, you must say what you normally wouldn't." Implicit in Mathews' claim is a belief in the merits of artistic and intellectual surprise: the capacity of a constrained work, in its inventive oddity, to unsettle, productively, audience and writer alike. For this reason, my book will be comprised of an extended series of exercises: essayistic trials, performed as a means of practice or training, whose outcomes are not predictable or foreordained. Designating the chapters as "exercises" is also intended to evoke the term's corporeal dimension, a notion — that literary constraint has bodily implications, even if only by analogy — that has become important in post-Oulipian conceptions of constraint. In short, the book's architectonic structure affords the exploratory space necessary for a critical praxis that values experimentation, uncertainty, and surprise.

Importantly, this creative-critical methodology acknowledges criticism as a species of performance, an acknowledgement made too infrequently in my view. As Benjamin Friedlander writes in his introduction to *Simulcast*, a work of literary criticism that experiments with plagiarism as a critical mode, "essays that flaunt their own literary qualities are often greeted with suspicion" within the realm of critical discourse (55). As in the philosophical realm, the decision to pay exaggerated attention to one's manner of presentation — the decision to "flaunt" the writing's literary qualities — often gets derided as coming at the cost of substance. Yet if constraints, however unapparent, are omnipresent in critical discourse, then to foreground their usage and increase their severity is to change the nature of the critical act only in degree, not in kind — is to exacerbate criticism's tendencies, not change them. Moreover, as literary theorists such as Stanley Fish have argued, to pretend that a zero degree writing style can be attained is itself a rhetorical posture. For his part, Friedlander goes even further when he asserts, "*Simulcast* suggests that the most suspicious writing of all *masks* its literary qualities" (55). Style is integral to substance (and vice versa): a lesson that literary criticism learned long ago with respect to its objects of study but has been much slower to apply to its own written praxis.

Constraint, defined

The *Concise Oxford English Dictionary* defines "constraint" as, simply, "a limitation or restriction." This terse, general definition of the term allows for a broad delineation of what constitutes literary constraint because almost any rule or factor intrinsic or extrinsic to the act of writing can be considered a limitation. Grammar, in this view, imposes constraints upon what constitutes acceptable word order. A lexicon constrains available word choice. Deadlines constitute constraints, as does the presence of collaborators. Even a writer's income or means of sustenance can be seen as a kind (or, in some cases, a lack) of constraint. This broad definition of the term reveals the ways in which all writing, done in whatever context, must obey explicit and implicit rules, reveals the way in which all writing is in some sense constrained.

The drawback of this broad definition is that it empties the category of literary constraint of any practical or theoretical significance, becoming just a synonym for "writing." In order, therefore, to make literary constraint a discrete, meaningful theoretical category, I define it according to its social practice and usage, rather than its metaphysical properties, and use the term to refer to texts that willfully inhabit what could be called the constraint-based tradition. This tradition begins with Oulipo in 1960 and stretches forward to include a host of present-day writers working under the sign or influence of the group, but also extends backwards in time to include unwitting precursors (what Oulipo playfully dubs "anticipatory plagiary": writing that plagiarized the group before it existed). With the exception of some anticipatory plagiary, all literary constraint announces itself as such, declares that it is imposing constraints upon itself over and above the constraints always present in the act of writing, and, thus, that it is participating in the tradition of Oulipo. As a rule, constraint-based writing craves self-reflexive attention, does not want its use of constraints to go overlooked or ignored, even when the author refuses to specify the nature of the constraints used.

Topics and Texts

This book will consider three principal groupings of writers: 1) founding, French, Oulipians; 2) English-language coevals of early Oulipians; 3) recent and contemporary instances of literary constraint, particularly from the United States and Canada. Because a preponderance of English-language literary constraint has been published in the past ten to twenty years, this last grouping, which constitutes the second and third generations of the constraint-based literary tradition, will be the book's focus. The first two groupings—the historical origins of the mode—will be surveyed predominantly for light they can shed on contemporary practices.

These groupings suggest an important question: Why has there been an efflorescence of North American constraint-based writing over the past decade or two? What makes this efflorescence all the more puzzling is that it has not happened, unlike Oulipo itself, as the result of a concerted literary movement, school, or group. Countless contemporary North American constraint-based writers declare their indebtedness to Oulipo, often in interviews, statements of poetics, prefaces and afterwords of books. Yet fewer of these writers declare similar levels of allegiance and influence to their peers' uses of constraint. Not only are these writers geographically scattered, but, most tellingly, there is, with a few exceptions that only prove the rule, no avowed spirit of togetherness pervasive among them. For Oulipo, the practice of constraint-based writing is first and foremost a collective endeavor, involving monthly meetings (which still take place to this day) as well as regular exchange and collaboration among participants. In its contemporary, North American context, literary constraint has by and large been practiced in relative isolation.

I argue that this shift in constraint-based practice subtly alters the nature of the texts produced: instead of viewing constraint as a playful literary laboratory experiment devoid of political ramifications, as Oulipians tend to do, contemporary English-language writers often view the practice as a form of cultural critique. Christian Bök, for example, dedicates his prominent constrained prose poem, Eunoia, to "the new ennui / in you," while Harryette Mullen's pop cultural alterations of canonical Shakespearean sonnets through a modified use of the N+7 technique suggest that rule-bound procedures can help us sift through and make sense of the vast field of cultural detritus that surrounds us. It is not that Bök, Mullen, and others see literary constraint as a handy antidote to individual feelings of loneliness, depression, or boredom, but, rather, that widespread loneliness, a more existential condition than isolation, produces a malaise, a "new ennui," that permeates the broader social, cultural, and political spheres.

The malaise these writers perceive stems from cultural excess: not only the sense that aspects of North American culture are extravagant and wasteful, but also the sense that the sheer quantity of available cultural material overwhelms the culture's participants. Mullen's poem "Jinglejangle," a long, alphabetical catalogue of vernacular sayings, provides a sense, through staggering linguistic variety, of the vastness of the American cultural terrain, as well as a sense of the way in which tawdry slogans and catchphrases permeate it. Similarly, the excessive eating, drinking, and sex in Bök's *Eunoia* cloys: characters routinely consume far-fetched food combinations, repulsive in their overabundant oddity, as when the narrator of "Chapter I" gorges himself on a "rich dish" consisting of "ribs with wings in chili" and "figs with kiwis in icing" (56). In both texts, unbridled freedom of choice figures as problematic: in the face of it, either paralysis ensues or, worse, overindulgence. Within such a context, constraint, rather than being an unpleasant form of coercion, becomes a helpful mechanism for navigating quantitative overload—becomes, paradoxically, liberating. Furthermore, within the context of a historical moment (the early- to mid-2000s) that saw the United States intent on exporting democracy, freedom, and "our way of life" to foreign peoples, willing or not, the decision to write using constraints must, I think, be seen as an implicit interrogation of the very concept of freedom. As British Oulipian Ian Monk has said, "One definition of freedom might be the ability to choose your own rules" (142).

I'd like to suggest, then, that the recent efflorescence of American constraint-based writing was no accident, but, rather, a response, even if unconscious, to prevailing anxieties about freedom and choice in our current historical moment, in the same way that the advent of Oulipo in 1960 can be seen as a subconscious response to French Existential thought of the 1940s and 1950s, itself a discourse deeply concerned with matters of freedom and choice. With this provisional answer as to why constraint has become widespread in recent English-language poetic and avant-garde praxis, the book will address what, exactly, the nature of these prevailing anxieties might be. The constraint in Doug Nufer's 2004 novel *Never Again*—no word in the book can be used twice—can be read, for example, as an allegory for, or an enactment of, the unchecked usage of natural resources. I am not claiming that Nufer set out to write an explicitly or dogmatically environmentalist novel (though the novel's narrator is in fact concerned about the hidden costs of widespread development), but that his chosen constraint resonates with concerns that are very much in the contemporary sociopolitical air, and, further, that self-imposed constraint presents a model, even if only allegorical, for curbing or delimiting authorial output, a model for avoiding some of the cultural excesses that trouble these writers.

Paradoxically, however, constraints produce their own form of excess: overheated rhetorical flights. The delimitation that constraints entail forces these writers' language in unexpected, fanciful directions, as in this description of an "erotic" dental hygienist's practices in Never Again: "Erotic entrepreneur hygienist nocturnally assignated patients desiring kinky dental care. Latexed fingertips, tightfit nurse's microskirt, sterile aromatics, pain-inducing instruments' latently sexualized perversions teased uptight jisms regular humping wouldn't unleash" (28). In this passage, just as the dental instruments tease out "uptight jisms regular humping wouldn't unleash," so too does the constraint itself tease out rapid-fire oddball locutions unconstrained writing wouldn't unleash. Such overblown rhetorical flights are the norm in many constraint-based texts—are, indeed, half their fun—which suggests that contemporary literary constraint is partly complicit with the excesses it critiques, is not only a diagnosis of a malaise but a symptom of it as well. With this difference: its excesses have a purgative effect. In a passage like the above, the improbable word-chains act like an emetic, poisoning the sentence with their awkward, strained grammar until they finally, from surfeit, effect a long-awaited rhetorical release. The texts, you could say, critique excess by farcically enacting it.

Of all the ways in which these texts enact excess, perhaps the most notable is their enactment of sex. Sexual passages and scenes occur far more frequently in contemporary English-language literary constraint than in its older, Oulipian predecessors. What's more, the sex scenes in the former, unlike those in the latter, tend to be raucous and outré, both in terms of the nature of the acts performed and in terms of the language used to render those acts. As the title of Mullen's collection *Sleeping with the Dictionary* suggests, for this second, post-Oulipian generation, writing with constraints is fundamentally erotic in nature: constrained language, with its tongue-strapping contortions, titillates, even when its content is not overtly sexual.

This shift in an understanding of constraint comes about, in my account, with the 1988 publication of Harry Mathews' *Singular Pleasures*, a collection of vignettes that inventively depict a variety of individuals masturbating. I read Mathews' depictions of masturbation as an allegory for the nature of literary constraint and argue that sex becomes such a crucial theme for subsequent generations of constraint-based writers because they worry that their writing practice is purely a matter of self-pleasure, with no broader social or political implications. These writers are wrestling with the question of what the rampant desire for self-pleasure—a desire they perceive, apprehensively, in the larger culture but nonetheless possess themselves—conceals. In grappling with this question, they are trying to find a way to make self-pleasure, in their writing, something more than mere self-indulgence, an ambition that, for many, necessitates a critique, one practically heretical to make in American political discourse, of the notion that complete freedom of choice is an unqualified good.

Introduction

: Context

Before I sat down to write the following introduction, I had no elaborate theoretical rationale for why it should be written in the form of an ad hoc recorded monologue other than that it seemed an easy way to get work done at a time when much wasn't happening. Whatever other rationales I invented in the moment of composition, what seems most notable to me now is the way such an introductory gesture undercuts the pretense of mastery that genres like the introduction and the prospectus rely upon. How to make an argument about the inadequacies of argument? One way to start is to write an introduction that doesn't quite introduce the book.

: What was I trying to do?

If, in this chapter and elsewhere, I put myself on the metaphorical (and actual) therapist's couch in order to write this book, then these prefatory reflections to each chapter not only provide context for the reader but are also a form of self-assessment before termination, a way of looking back at the project and providing closure. Part of me feels embarrassed by all these self-involved gestures, but another part suspects that it's this aspect of the project — the way it foregrounds academic work as an indirect means of self-exploration — in which its essential originality consists.

Introduction

August 7, 2010
3:15 P.M.

this book had its beginnings in a workshop   about three or four years ago   at the CUNY Graduate Center   where I'm a student in the English PhD program   it was called a "Dissertation Workshop" but it was actually more a professionalization workshop   where instead of coming in each week and exchanging dissertation chapters let me rephrase that   strike that last   I'm not sure how this is going to work exactly but I'd imagine   compared to other writing I've done this way   that is   talking into a voice recorder   I'm going to edit afterwards a lot more   I'm writing this way   why am I writing this way   first I find it easier than actual writing   easier to write though harder to write well this way   but I'm willing to make that sacrifice for the sake of getting the work done   but second   and equally as important   this kind of rambling associative monologue has something to do with the personal nature of my project   that is it's as though I'm putting myself on the therapist's couch   I'm actually lying down on a couch now   and trying to diagnose where this project came from   why I undertook it   but the point I want to make is that   I don't think the intellectual origins of this book can be separated from its personal origins   in other words   the intellectual rationale for the project is not a pure clean one   a matter of argumentative necessity   the project arises instead out of my temperament and beliefs   and that's important because while many academic projects have a clear basis in the personality the background and the life of the author   the scholar has to write   has to mute those personal origins   has to write as though those personal reasons weren't the motivation for the book   to make it seem that the motivation comes from purely discursive and argumentative reasons   the personal motivations alone aren't sufficient   and in my project   the personal motivations   if they're not sufficient   which they may well not be   they're nonetheless primary   and not being disavowed   there are intellectual reasons for my project   and I'll lay some of them out as

I go   but ultimately   as I'm nearing the end   it seems more and more personal than I initially realized   I don't know   this all sounds clumsier than I'd like   it will be hard to spontaneously   this is an example of a point that suffers from not being written out where it could be articulated more thoroughly   more airtight   anyway the point I want to make is that my project takes it as axiomatic that [phone rings] not only   oh Jesus   phone going off   [phone rings]   hello   hey how's it going   yeah I'm working   no no I just started   yeah probably another hour or two   where are you   well do you do you want   yeah I'd like to go biking when I'm done with this   it won't be for at least another hour though   so yeah   what time do you want to go   I don't know let me check the weather   let me check when sunset is   where do they have it on here   "Details" you think   here it is   sunset at 8:04   so why don't we plan on going at seven   yeah sounds good   let's say seven   and figure you get home by six-thirty or so   I don't I don't know   we can eat together if you want   just give me another couples of hours   okay sounds good   see you later   okay   sorry about that interruption   it was Shari   and actually the interruption was appropriate because it was a personal phone call   Shari being my wife   so the point I wanted to make was   I don't think scholarship would be better or worse with or without the personal included in it   but that my project suggests that the inclusion of the personal might be a slightly more honest way of doing it   or [sigh] it's hard to set it up as non-hierarchical   or not value-laden   these claims   so maybe the way to say it would be that the inclusion of the personal in scholarship   is an alternative   a generally unacknowledged alternative   one that's not at this point in time by and large considered licit   which proscription I think closes off certain interpretive possibilities   I'm certainly not opposed to traditional scholarship   am not trying to hack at its legs and cut it down into something else although I will say   I do tend to find a lot of academic criticism not only difficult to endure but also not particularly useful or informative   that said   scholarship that is useful and informative   an example   a book that for whatever reason   probably because I know the author   he teaches at the Graduate Center   is David Reynolds' *Beneath the American Renaissance*   and I remember reading it and thinking   this is what criticism is supposed to do   the book was a magisterial work of historical restoration   placing the canonical writers of the American Renaissance in their historical context   in the context of popular literature of the time   dominant cultural strains   and so forth   and it was just this prodigious effort   measured in a crude way by the sheer size of the book   that took a topic I knew a fair bit about   and completely illuminated it in ways that hadn't been done before   though I do recall   thinking about it   a conversation with David in his office   early on in grad school where I was expressing my dissatisfaction with the conventions of academic writing   and he told me that I reminded him a bit of himself when he was starting out   but that he came around to realize scholarship is a kind of game   and that if you want to play it you eventually learn how to play by its rules   which ultimately I've refused to do   but so   let me go back now   and I think I'm going to stop lying down   and will instead walk about my apartment like I do when I'm on a phone call I'm excited about   so anyway I was taking this dissertation workshop   and in terms of practical nuts and bolts information about how to navigate the university profession   this was by far the most useful and valuable experience I've had in grad school   it was a tremendously practical course   and as I was saying   the students didn't just come in and exchange dissertation chapters   the course covered all aspects of professionalization   how to write an effective CV   how to decipher job ads   how to write a dissertation prospectus   all sorts of pointers that you'd have a hard time getting   getting all in one place at any rate   so I'm taking this course   and as useful as I'm making it sound   it actually threw me into my first of two minor life crises in graduate school   the crisis pertained specifically to anxieties I had about professionalization   simply put   and I realize there are problems with this position   it seems to me more a vocation than a profession   that the very notion of being a literary professional seemed somehow oxymoronic or absurd or against the very spirit of the enterprise   it's like poker   another activity I'm marginally professional at   what does it mean to be a professional poker player   I guess the most obvious definitions hinge on economics   you make a living off the game   so I'll grant that it's possible to be a literary professional   and in many ways I am one myself   but professionalization goes to such an extreme in a certain narrow direction   that as an intellectual slash artist slash whatever I am   I couldn't imagine wanting to do it on those terms   didn't want to claim that identity and further   the workshop made it starkly apparent that the things I was going to have to do in order to professionalize were things I was loath to do   in other words   I was headed down a career path   and you could say "well you should know this before going into a PhD program"   but the passage of so much time is involved   and who you are at each point is so different   that it's impossible to predict where the process is going to take you   actually for our school newspaper I wrote an essay evaluating the humanities PhD as a kind of wager   or gamble   looking at it from a risk assessment point of view   and of course it's a terrible bet from that point of view   the other thing the weird thing that happened to me as I went through graduate school   it started out as a hobby   but over time I got good enough at it that I could make significantly more money playing online poker than I could teaching   which is as much a commentary on an adjunct's salary as it is my poker prowess   so I became a kind of part-time professional poker player   which at points interfered with my schoolwork   that was the subsequent crisis I had after the one I haven't finished talking about   but anyway   backtracking when I say I was loath to professionalize   what I mean is I didn't want to write the kind of work that academic discourse encourages not just encourages   requires   the professoriate to write   in order to be credentialed as expert   get tenure and so forth   that the majority of refereed academic journals and the articles in them I mean I'm not against scholarship per se   there's loads of wonderful scholarship that gets done   but the current system seems designed to turn out a lot of second-rate work that I find it hard to get excited about   and I don't mean that criticism needs to constantly shock and thrill   reading Kant thrills me   so it's not about a certain level of entertainment or excitement value   it's about intellectual stimulation   and grappling with things in a way that makes them seem like they matter   I don't know   I'm getting carried away   the point is   and actually another important aspect of the personal intellectual history that I'm trying to recount   is that I had these feelings well before I entered graduate school   and I'd actually like to go a little further back in time   because this seems important when I was an undergraduate I took a couple of electives on essay writing with Pat Hoy   the Director of the Expository Writing Program at NYU   who's a dynamic engaging orator   but also a stern no-nonsense professor   I've met few other teachers more capable of getting the best possible work out of every student in the class   and Pat attended West Point   and ended up having to serve   reluctantly   as an officer in Vietnam   after he left the military   he went to graduate school to study literature   and I don't want to speak on behalf of Pat   but as I understand it when he began sending out pieces of his dissertation for publication he realized that his academic work didn't bear the stamp of who he was as a person   what he had experienced in and around the war   it was almost a suppression or effacement of his experiences   which is fine I guess   scholarship doesn't need a personality to do what it does   but the work somehow seemed less vital   well   again   I think I'm speaking more for myself here than for Pat   but this is a long way of saying that given my age when I studied with him   and given how great a teacher he is   Pat had a big influence on me   and I was taking these essay writing classes   and in them he basically taught us to write as writers and not as academics   a distinction that   again   is really my own not Pat's   but it's an insight I first had through him   even if most academics wouldn't be flattered by this notion   and it is an unflattering one   but I think it's true too   I don't know   I'm making lots of tenuous claims   well   in Pat's case   what he went on to realize was that there was a disconnect   geez   I'm really putting a lot of words in his mouth   ventriloquizing him because I know him and his work so well   it's like when you're teaching and you say   in response to a student question   "well I think Kant would argue"   and you assume   on the basis of what you know about Kant   what Kant would say if faced with that exact question   but anyway   there was this disconnect between the highly concentrated academic work Pat was doing on E. M. Forster and what his broader experience in the world had been   and so he started writing these personal essays   about soldiering   about West Point   things based on personal experience   and the essays would draw on his literary background and learning   but they were always firmly rooted in the personal   but so   even as an undergraduate   I had these certain vague   partially formed notions about trying to live a life that was engaged with literature but that wasn't operating in the ruts of academic discourse   and yet   at the same time   I wanted the work I was doing   and maybe this applies more to my work now   in graduate school   I wanted the work to have some sort of relationship to scholarly discourse   what I didn't want was the taint of dilettantism or amateurism   the idea that you could only be doing serious scholarship in this exact way   that   for example   if you were writing the introduction to your book by pacing back and forth in your bedroom and talking into a voice recorder that it may be more or less interesting as an experiment   but it's not serious scholarship   I think that's emphatically false   I think what I'm doing here has as much intellectual integrity as any of the more conventional ways of writing scholarship   it's funny   the things I'm recollecting as I talk are not things I thought of   or imagined as all that relevant   as I've worked on this project over the past three years   but now that I'm talking aloud   and not writing   that background seems like such a natural arc or progression   that not mentioning them would be a disservice   it's not that mentioning them is ethically irresponsible   irresponsible would be doing it the other way   to pretend that none of this came out of this decade-long process of personal-intellectual growth   and I certainly don't claim uniqueness in this regard   what I'm doing here is what anyone writing an academic book could do   to trace its origins in this way   what's unique is that I'm making the gambit and doing it   dreading what it's going to sound like when I transcribe this   but for now I feel inspired and somewhat justified   okay   so I had this background   and entering graduate school I wanted to study the essay as a literary form   and actually what I've done is instead of studying it   I'm practicing it   my project   from this point of view   is basically an attempt to write as many different kinds of essays as possible   so I'm not writing about the essay   but trying to write scholarship essayistically   as a trial   and everything such a term would imply   so with that rough background   I'm taking this dissertation workshop and I have this crisis regarding professionalization specifically it dawns on me that my current projected   I'm being encouraged from a few different quarters to write about Native American literature   American poets who have written about Native American cultures in the twentieth century   and obviously the topic interests me   but it wasn't work   I mean I specifically had this realization when I went to a conference on Native American literature and I actually had a great experience there   the people I met were friendly   there was interesting work being done   good conversations that were happening   but being around other scholars and writers working in the field   I realized that my relation to it   I couldn't ever feel the level of connection that they felt to it   my interest felt a little touristic   it would have been a course of study that (sigh) at a certain point in my life I would have been going through the motions   I always would have been doing it in part because it would probably give me a slightly better chance at getting a job   and taking the dissertation workshop intensified this sentiment   I started to feel that I was doing certain things in my intellectual life purely because of how they would situate me to get a job   and not because I wanted to be doing them   and you know that's the definition of a job   that you have to do things you don't want to do   but not only did I have these anxieties   and midway through the workshop I sort of shut down and couldn't do any schoolwork whatsoever   reading   writing   nothing   not only did I have these anxieties   I started to have a train of thought that went something like this   I got into literature and tried to make a life or career out of it   or something in between   because I liked doing it   I had started college in the business school   but it didn't take long for me to develop intellectual interests   before college I didn't read or write much and suddenly I really started to enjoy doing those things   so the reasons for studying the humanities were very clear to me   I passed up a course of study where the financial rewards are very obvious   business school   which was an important reason why I even went to NYU in the first place   I mean I got a small scholarship there but not particularly much   it was on the margins of what my family could afford   we both took out loans   my parents and I   and I reasoned   well I'll go into debt   but when I get out   I'll make a decent amount of money and will be able to pay it off without much worry   the point being   it was a very clear trade-off for me   in terms of what to study   between the financial viability of it   and the enjoyment of it   so now I'm sitting here   I'm having this crisis   and I think   if I'm going to continue on and get a PhD in literature   the only way in which it's worth doing is if at every step of the way I act idealistically   that is   I only do things based on whether or not I want to do them   and not out of a sense of obligation   or because it will get me a job   here was my reasoning and I'm not saying it's not flawed   but I felt that if I was going to do things that I didn't like or that I felt lukewarm about   or that were unpleasant   then I may as well not get a PhD at all   that the only reason to get a PhD in the humanities was because you were doing something you like   work-wise   if I was going to do something I didn't like   I'd at least do something that made me real money   I don't know   maybe the poker money I started making was going to my head a bit   but it just seemed that in academia the payoff was too unlikely   in terms of the likelihood of getting a job   and even if I were to get one   tenured or not   the rewards were likely still too paltry   the sacrifices too large   to make it worth doing anything other than exactly what I wanted to be doing as a scholar   as an academic   as a person   at the same time that I had this realization   that the way for me to go through graduate school in the humanities was as an uncompromising idealist   and there are problems with this position   but I do believe it's a useful corrective to the careerist pressures that have only escalated in the past decade   anyway   at the same time that I'm having this crisis   indifferent to school-related things   what I was doing at that time   in my own personal reading   there was creeping over my consciousness that the only things I wanted to do in relation to reading and writing were things that thrilled me   things that I just absolutely enjoyed   and that sounds like an obvious thing to say   who doesn't want to read things they enjoy   but it's a hard principle to follow when you're studying something   study by its nature saps some of the vitality from what you're studying   but so at this time   most of the reading I was doing was about Oulipo and constraint   Oulipo being a group of mathematicians and writers   founded in 1960   with the goal of inventing constraints that could be used to generate literary texts   so I was reading stuff by Oulipo   I had previously taught Georges Perec's *Species of Spaces and Other Pieces*   which isn't strictly Oulipian   but it's a literary sensibility that felt very close to my heart   weirdly austere and distant   and yet somehow affecting and touching   poignant and perceptive   in a way I was just following up on my interest in this one book   and I was also doing a little of my own writing with the use of constraints   writing poems on the subway and so forth   so I was having these thoughts about the importance of pleasure   I haven't used that word in this introduction yet   but it's an important word for me   in both my pedagogy and in my reading and writing   so I was having these intuitions about the centrality of pleasure to literary study at the same time that I was taking an immense pleasure in this mode of writing just for its own sake   and so what suggested itself to me was   if I was going to only study things that I really liked   why not work on Oulipo   and in keeping with my prior intuitions about the nature of academic writing   about essayism as a more supple mode of intellectual inquiry   the most logical idea suggested itself   which was that not only would I write about constraint   and I couldn't write about Oulipo specifically because my French isn't good enough   but I'm glad actually   because I think Oulipo's legacy is the more interesting topic at this point in time   English-language writing that's broadly in the tradition of the group   and that's what this project is about   I mean this introduction is really   it's not much of an introduction in that it doesn't frame what the project is about but how I arrived at it   maybe I'll have to write a second introduction   like Oulipian Marcel Bénabou in his *Why I Have Not Written Any of My Books*   in which the first several chapters are prefaces where he keeps starting over   he writes chapter one and he says no no no no no   chapter two begins he says no no no   chapter one was all wrong   this is the actual beginning of the book   and then chapter three comes and he says I've failed yet again   here's how I'm going to start   he sort of performs his nervousness and anxiety about writing by continually beginning again   which is a very Oulipian gesture   anyway   the idea I had was that not only was I going to write about literary constraint   I was going to do so using constraints   my dissertation would itself be constraint-based   and one rationale for this approach   beyond just the principle of self-pleasure   is that criticism is the one area of creative endeavor   and notice I'm describing criticism as a creative endeavor   it's the one area of creative endeavor Oulipo hasn't explored   using constraints not to write a novel or poem but to say something critically substantial   so that's what this project is   and I guess the question at this point isn't how to describe the project   since it seems pretty apparent that this introduction won't quite do that   the question then becomes   what can I say or conclude   let me try to put it less grandly   I've recounted some of the personal intellectual origins of this project   what might it indicate   about the project itself   about criticism   why is this background relevant   I guess that's kind of the same question but that's to say   well here's how I'm going to attempt to answer the question   I haven't really posed a question   but maybe the answer will suggest what the question would have been had I been more articulate   I had the idea to write the introduction this way after re-reading Ben Friedlander's introduction to Simulcast   which is a work of literary criticism that experiments with plagiarism as a critical mode   and what struck me about re-reading his introduction which I hadn't noticed the first time I read the book   was how personal in nature it is   his introduction is about fifty to sixty pages long   in what is maybe a 200- or 250-page-long book   so you can tell just by the length of the introduction that Friedlander feels a defense of his project needs to be made   and I understand why he feels that way   given the strangeness of what he's doing   and also given the intricacies of his project   some of what he wrote was inflammatory within poetry communities when it first appeared   so he addresses those controversies and the ethics of what he was doing   so he's writing this defense of his project   but when I first read his arguments   I found them so gripping that I failed to notice how rooted they are in the personal   I specifically remember   in my rereading a passage where he mentioned his skateboard   and I thought "who would admit   in a work of scholarship   that he used to ride a skateboard"   in other words   it's not just an academic argument he's making about what criticism is and isn't   the argument he's making is about how he grew up as a scholar   as an intellectual and as a poet   and has everything to do with who he is as a person   that those two things   the intellectual and the personal   are inseparable   and that to shroud the personal in intellectual justifications   again I don't want to put value judgments on it and say it's bad   that would be too simplistic   but not hiding the personal makes it I think a different project   and changes its tenor   implicit in Friedlander's book   in other words   is an argument that who one is in the world   and how one interacts with and relates to others in the world   has everything to do with the ideas that one puts forth in writing   scholars by nature are actually very naturally constrained obeying an elaborate   almost bureaucratic   system of discipline and rules   protocols   and these issues relate to the contents of Friedlander's book and the fact that some of his essays were originally written pseudonymously   and the fact that the essays attempt a social mapping of various experimental poetic communities   and I'm reminded too   maybe this will be where I wrap up   I remember when I began this project   talking to Wayne Koestenbaum   who said something that stuck with me   that at the time I didn't exactly have the context or experience to be able to grasp its full import   he said something to the effect of   "find as many ways as possible to bring your work out into the world   to make your project part of some sort of larger social fabric"   and I can't say at this point I've done that in any widespread way   which is fine   but the ways in which my project has experienced nodes of connectivity   even if only to other individuals who have sustained and nourished my thinking   has been vital   I think Wayne framed it   I think he said something along the lines of   when you're doing something this strange   you don't want to feel like it's just you   like you're totally in outer space   and you're doing this really bizarre project   and it has no relation to anything   because   implicit in that point   is that when you've abandoned certain safety nets   and maybe I have others in place   listing them here isn't the point   but that if I had written a dissertation on American poets and Native American cultures in the twentieth century   even if I had never shown a word of it to anyone   I would still feel like I was in conversation with previous scholars and with the discipline   and so there's a way in which you wouldn't be as out there   yeah I mean   am I just saying if you're out there you need other people   that's a little simplistic   you need other people even if you're not out there   well I've definitely lost my momentum at this point   I've arrived at a sheer cliff-face   I guess what I'd say is   that the risk for this project   is now   and always has been   that I'd be trying to have a conversation with the discipline   and the discipline wouldn't be interested in listening   and then the question becomes   why is it if I've abandoned all these conventions   why is it that I feel that having a conversation with the discipline is so important   and the answer to that   well if I have a good answer to that I'm golden   but the simple answer might be that I also love rules   find them comforting in the way I imagine well-behaved scholars must   the more grandiose answer might be that reading and writing are profoundly imaginative tasks   and consequently   one's own practices of them need to be every bit as imaginatively engaged as the work under consideration   even for critics   I mean   so what   am I just saying   critics   well you know what   I'll try to end here I've been trying to end for ten minutes   but I'm not having much luck   because obviously I would like a thunderous ending   earlier I said that I view criticism as creative   and to go back to another moment in my past   I can recall the first literature class I ever took   an Intro to Lit course at NYU   and at the end of the semester   the professor   a grad student   one of the ones who're cute in their shy quaintness and sincerity   said something that I think meant something different to her than it did to me then and than it does to me now   but it was a notion that always ignited my imagination   and that was   she said   maybe it's possible to view literary criticism itself as a kind of art   and that idea   I don't just mean it looks pretty   I mean that the argumentation itself can have a kind of elegance   that in order to be able to make the argument that *Beneath the American Renaissance* does   it requires a profound and capacious act of imagination   is that where I want to end   of course not   I don't want to end   but   here's where I'll end   and here I really will end   I think what my professor more or less meant when she talked about literary criticism as an art   is take pride in your craft   I don't know what she meant   who knows   but I'm confident she was writing regular academic prose   and incidentally when I was reading up on the art critic Dave Hickey   I saw that he teaches at UNLV   and then I saw that my former lit professor was now teaching there as well   and I wondered how she liked having him as a colleague   what would she make of what the rebellious Dave Hickey does with his criticism   with his life   but it was just a weird coincidence to see that she teaches there now and to realize she has an existence beyond just the class I took with her over ten years ago   it was like when I saw my history professor in the supermarket   my first semester of college   we were both buying beer and I was completely startled by it   not by the fact that she was buying beer or that I was under-aged and buying beer   but that there she was on a Gristede's check-out line   out in the world   anyway what I find particularly suggestive   I was thinking about the artfulness of literary criticism in relation to this recent movement called conceptual poetry   and conceptual poetry involves a lot of appropriation   and Kenny Goldsmith   the most prominent conceptual poet   makes the point that the simple act of moving information from one place to another is   in our culture   a prominent form of writing   is a creative act   and that's a lot of what his artistic practice involves   moving information from one place to another   and the revelation for me thinking about this notion in the context of criticism was that that's what criticism has always done from its inception   it takes information from one place   a book   a movie   a poem   and moves it somewhere else and in changing the context of that information has tried to make it into something else   has tried to make it sing even if only argumentatively   arguably too   it's not just in quoting a text that criticism moves information   but it moves information in the sense that   and I know certain critics don't buy into this notion   but in the sense that there's a latent level of meaning there's a meaning behind the words   that's implicit in them   and criticism takes that level of meaning and moves it to the forefront   it's foregrounding it and making it apparent   so it's not just moving the texts themselves and changing their context   it's changing the context of how the texts signify   doing something with the texts' meanings   moving those meanings around   and so in a weird way the Conceptual practice of information transferal   well of course it's been done before   it's been done for centuries   there's often an historical amnesia in their pronouncements about their practice   which I suppose is an inevitable part of avant-garde posturing   but what I think is most germane   aside from what it suggests about criticism as a kind of stealth artistic practice   and I've always felt   as a writer   that I like working off the ideas of others better than I do just creating something myself out of the void   so I like the idea of criticism as a stealth art   but the last point I'll make   is that if conceptual poetry has these affinities with criticism   as practices   it suggests that conceptual poetry itself is a kind of critical practice   that maybe   you could say   the major breakthrough of conceptual poetry as an art practice   is that it blurs the boundaries between criticism and art in a way never quite so completely done before   and its focus on a "thinkership" as opposed to an readership   a clumsy term but one conceptual poets have advanced   supports this idea   in other words   conceptual poetry does something critical   it changes the context of an object   and therefore its meaning   and lets you see it in a way that you otherwise wouldn't have   and in so doing it makes art   or   even more precisely   the Conceptual framing gesture   which is fundamentally a critical gesture   a kind of reading of a text   the precise way to say it is   that conceptual poetic practice implies that any reading of a text is   fundamentally   an act of artistic creation

Anticipatory Plagiary

Raymond Roussel's (New) Africa

: Context

French poet, novelist, playwright, chess enthusiast, neurasthenic, and drug addict Raymond Roussel is perhaps the most important anticipatory plagiarist of — which is to say, influence on — Oulipo. In his masterpiece of obscurantism, *New Impressions of Africa*, a poem in four cantos, the primary plot of each canto consists of a straightforward description of a site in Egypt. The description has scarcely begun when a parenthesis opens, introducing a digression. Soon a second parenthesis interrupts the first digression with another digression, then a third parenthesis opens, a fourth, a fifth. Amid these embedded digressions, footnotes soon intrude, each containing their own internal parentheses. As the canto approaches its end, the parentheses are closed in succession, each closure hurtling the confused reader back into the suspended grammar of the previous sentence.

: What was I trying to do?

Like Roussel himself, I was trying, through unrestrained digression, to avoid monochrome argumentation. Not having a point, I now realize, is not all that hard to accomplish. What's more difficult is doing it well, so well, in fact, that you end up having one after all.

Raymond Roussel's (New) Africa

Raymond Roussel's 1932 book-length poem *New Impressions of Africa* contains parentheses (The effect is like a Russian nesting doll ((Or perhaps it is like *Tristram Shandy*, that masterpiece of digression (((How thrilling are digressions within digressions! ((((How thrilling is recursiveness!)))) It is as if the mind delights at the prospect of never arriving at a telos ((((Imagine, for example, hiking in unmarked woods (((((Meaning there are no trails or paths which you can follow.))))) and becoming lost. You hadn't intended to wander far from your campsite, but first one thing, then another, has led you astray (((((In succession: a quaint pond, several hundred yards behind the campsite; a massive boulder, on the other side of the pond; an enticing kaleidoscope of sunlight piercing the tree line; the ghastly underbelly of a large, uprooted tree; a disarmingly lush fern patch.))))). Suddenly, an hour later, you look around, standing amid a sea of fern, and realize that you don't know your way back to the campsite. You think it might be to the south—or what you assume to be the south, anyway—but you're not sure. Each direction looks the same: ferns afoot and, as far as you can see, a smattering of frighteningly nondescript, toothpick-like trees. A warm sensation of terror slowly descends upon you. You don't know to what extent you're in danger, but you know that you are in it (((((*If I walk in the wrong direction, you wonder, just how far does this forest continue?*))))). Your enraptured wandering has put you at considerable risk. Now, if you had been a writer (((((Composing a poem about your impressions of Africa, say.))))) and divagated similarly with words, the risks, comparatively, would be nugatory (((((When, only ten lines in to *New Impressions*, Roussel swerves[1] off course, and then swerves away from his initial swerve, frustrated readers are at liberty to put down the book and resume the business of their day or, better yet, to continue reading and luxuriate in the tangents. Either way, they face no grave danger from his Byzantine peregrinations.))))). Digressions, in other words, allow for safe, controlled (((((Constraints induce a severe, rough-and-tumble dialectic between control and wildness. Every constraint-based writer knows that we are least in control when we are most in control ((((((Or something like that)))))).))))) thought-adventure. If we must think of digressions as swerves (((((Delightful word, that: it literally swerves off the tongue.))))), let us cast aside the term's pejorative connotations and instead understand swerving as a healthy, cathartic action.[2] We swerve to prolong tension, to make the return voyage sweeter. We swerve in prose because we do so as easily in real life[3] (((((In his essay "How I Wrote Certain of my Books," Roussel declares that from his extensive travels ((((((He was born into a wealthy family.)))))), "I never took anything for my books" ((((((p. 20)))))). He declares this because he believes "it clearly shows just how much imagination accounts for everything in my work." Perhaps, if he is to be believed ((((((Remember D. H. Lawrence's dictum: "Never trust the artist. Trust the tale."))))))), but it also demonstrates that Roussel understood writing as a defiant swerve away from the world of actuality.))))).)))), at the prospect of eschewing purposiveness ((((Purposive purposelessness, Kant called it. Or was it the other way around? That art should aspire to such a condition seems effete, ineffectual. Aren't we supposed to be changing the world for the better? Unmasking the insidious power structures that govern our lives? (((((This is another question I quaver to address. Not for reasons of space, but because I doubt ever being able to answer it satisfactorily. It is, though, a specter that haunts Oulipian practice, at least in critics' eyes: How to justify their participation in the art for art's sake tradition? Without attempting to answer the question ((((((I'll make one attempt: In an interview, film director Elia Suleiman (((((((Director, among other things, of *Divine Intervention*, a work of pro-Palestinian agitprop.))))))) was asked what he understood the political role of art to be. He replied that the

1 Thus: Anything else might date from yesterday:
The name whose proud yet crushed bearer can say
From memory, straight off and without fail
(As the occupant, by the topmost rail
Of a high block, in airy garret, knows—
A photographer skilled in hiding crows'
Feet and pimples with wily stratagems—
((Art of retouching! As, decked out in gems
(((Each, when having a proud photo taken
Of his beloved self, will stand unshaken

(And so on ((I include this quote more to provide the flavor of a typical passage from the poem than to illustrate an important point or idea contained within it. The poem continues on for 125 more pages in this vein. It is, from a practical standpoint, unreadable (((By claiming Roussel as an important forebear, Oulipo situates its writing praxis at the borderland of readability ((((Raymond Queneau's *100,000,000,000,000,000 Poems* (((((A series of 10 sonnets with interchangeable lines, thus yielding 10^{14}, or 100,000,000,000,000,000, potential poems ((((((Queneau calculated that it would take a person reading the poem twenty-four hours a day 190,258,751 years to finish it.)))))).))))) is the paradigmatic example of an unreadable Oulipian poem.)))). It is not that the **Oulipo** aims to create texts that cannot be read in their entirety, or texts that tax the patience of readers, but that they delight in the creation of dense, knotty structures. Theirs is an aesthetic of frustration and bedazzlement—an aesthetic, in a word, of the pointless raised to the status of the exalted ((((I am really getting carried away best art, the best cultural production, makes its audience want to go out in the world as better people—it uplifts and invigorates. In other words, art can change the world, but only indirectly, obliquely, by transforming individual attitudes. Coming from such an artist (((((((that is, someone whose films are directly motivated by a political agenda))))))), I find this account of how art performs cultural work convincing: he has no delusions that his film will single-handedly liberate Palestine—it performs its political work at the level of individual consciousness.)))))), I'd note that critics are much more concerned about the question of the Oulipo's literary politics than about the question of Roussel's ((((((*The* n*oulipian Analects,* a recent critical compilation concerning the legacy of Oulipian practice on contemporary Anglophone poetics, contains numerous essays that address the question of Oulipo's politics, all of which wonder, in essence: *What exactly are they and why is Oulipo so silent about them?* Formal radicalism, however, does not ipso facto imply political radicalism. Just because the Oulipo's writing practices are artistically avant-garde does not mean that their politics must be loud and progressive as well. In point of fact, as many critics in the Analects note, numerous Oulipians are, or have been, involved in progressive political movements and most seem sympathetic to progressive causes. What troubles the critics, then, it seems, is that members of the group never explicitly link their artistic practices to their political beliefs and actions.)))))). It is as if the apolitical nature of Roussel's literary practice can be excused as the workings of a

here. I have no idea what I mean by that.)))).))). For example, Oulipian Ian Monk explains in his "Introduction" to *New Impressions* that in the poem's long second canto, "608 lines separate the subject of the initial sentence from its main verb" (((p. 5))). No reader can juggle the thread of that sentence (((And as the primary sentence of the canto, it is presumably the most important one: all the others are subsidiary, asides ((((Though it hardly needs pointing out that for Roussel (((((as well as for myself))))) the asides are the point (((((What sort of aesthetic might that suggest? I quaver to broach the question within this already bloated footnote.))))).)))).))) as they read through the second canto.)) it goes.)

2 The clinamen (I always wonder ((Other things I wonder: Where do porn stars come from and how do they ((((whoever they may be))) find so many different people to perform in pornography? Why must happiness be fleeting? Should I stay or should I go?)): Am I the only person who thinks "clinamen" sounds like a dirty word ((The astute reader will have observed (((Like Auguste Dupin in "The Murders in the Rue Morgue."))) that my feelings about the dirtiness of the clinamen are what led me to articulate my wonderment about porn stars (((Porn stars are definitely a swerve.))).))?), an important concept in Oulipian and 'Pataphysical practice, comes from the Greek *klesis*, "a bending," and denotes those moments in a text when the author disobeys the rules of a constraint for aesthetic reasons.

3 This, incidentally, is the essayist's credo.

bourgeois eccentric, whereas Oulipo's literary practice, because collective, must spell out some sort of larger political program.))))). For myself, at least, it is enough that art brings a modicum of thoughtful pleasure into my life, whatever tectonic changes it may or may not effect upon the larger world.)))).))), delayal and interruption (((*New Impressions*, you could say[4], enacts a poetics of interruptions: a poetics aimed at thwarting readers' habits and desires (((((I return to the question of what sort of aesthetic this poetics implies. Obviously, one that considers postponement integral to pleasure (((((This quality alone argues for the importance of New Impressions in today's world, a world drunk on the internet's velocity.))))). Less obviously, it is an aesthetic that craves readership (((((Roussel, it is well known, was convinced his writing would secure him an exalted posthumous reputation.))))), challenging readers to stick with the text, in spite of all its excesses, to affirm, tacitly, by turning page after page, the merit of the poem. Whatever else it may be, artistic difficulty is almost always a come on, coyly flattering its audience's discerning judgment and taste.)))).))) and horseplay, that incomparable romp through the possibilities of the book.)), in that each successive doll seems, somehow, more and more improbable. Until finally, after peeling away countless layers of this strange onion, the last nub of a doll emerges, smooth, waxy, smiling, a tiny nugget of color as splendid in its own way as any of its bulkier kinfolk.) embedded within one another.[5]

---

4 Some strategies that Roussel employs to this end (in addition, of course, to the rampant use of parenthetical asides): footnotes (From Ian Monk's "Introduction" to *New Impressions*: "The role of the footnotes works exactly the same way as the parentheses, in other words they interrupt the linear reading of the book, and it is not always easy to see why Roussel decided to choose one or the other solution at a given moment, since some footnotes could easily be new parentheses ((Indeed, the footnotes even respect the rhyme and meter of the main poem.)) and vice versa" ((p. 9)).), interpolated illustrations, (Drawn by H.-A. Zo.) and the very shape of the physical book itself (The tops of the pages containing the illustrations remain uncut, which forces the reader to either cut them before reading or to peer underneath them to the extent possible while reading.).

5 Gutted of their digressions, the primary sentences of *New Impressions*' three cantos are (like my own primary sentence) frightfully mundane. The primary sentence of Canto II:

> Merely to cite him joining in combat,
> At an age when his coat and *little* hat —
> The full-length greatcoat — from which each construes
> A daunting aura, whatever his views —
> _____
> _____ *(The parentheses begin here.)*
> Still on that last sheer rock his uniform
> Had not begun to magnify his form,
> Means, pensive, we forget for a moment
> Egypt, its evenings, sun and firmament.

(In other words, what the poem "forgets," what its far-ranging digressions and asides occlude, is Africa itself, and the author's impressions of it ((I leave it to better (((less mischievous?))) minds than mine own to determine how problematic this textual eclipse is, and whether or not we get something — if not finer, then equally exotic (((This word obviously has pejorative colonialist connotations in this context, but I use it nonetheless. At bottom, *New Impressions of Africa* is a text about the exoticism of digressions ((((This topic — the colonialist implications of digression in *New Impressions* — deserves an essay in its own right. Should anyone ever see fit to write such an essay, I permit them to insert it here (((((INSERT ESSAY HERE.))))), provided, of course, it's any good.)))), a text about the allure and the perils of the unknown.))), in its stead.)).)

Reading *I Remember*

: Context

Joe Brainard was an artist and writer associated with the New York School, whose prodigious and innovative body of work includes assemblages, collages, drawing, and painting, as well as designs for book and album covers, theatrical sets and costumes. He is perhaps best known for his 1970 book *I Remember*, which radically departs from the conventions of the traditional memoir. It is neither chronological nor thematic; rather, each sentence begins "I remember . . ." and is followed by a single memory delivered with uniform weight and declaration. His deft juxtapositions of the banal with the revelatory, the very particular with the seemingly universal accumulate into a complex portrait of his childhood in the '40s and '50s in Oklahoma as well as his life as an artist and gay man in '60s and '70s New York.

: What was I trying to do?

As in the previous chapter, and as in many of the chapters that follow, this chapter operates by means of mimicry, adopting the basic form of Brainard's *I Remember* in order to write about it. Distinct from imitation, which has as its goal fidelity to the original such that the copy could potentially be mistaken for it, mimicry inflects the person or thing being copied with the personality of the mimic. The goal of this inflection is not, as in caricature, distortion, or exaggeration. Rather, it stems from the mimic's desire, like the little boy putting on his father's shoes, to express himself while inhabiting someone else's persona—by inhabiting someone else's persona. The risk, as with all acting, is that the actor's self-regard may usurp the role.

Reading *I Remember*

I remember reading Joe Brainard's *I Remember*, an autobiography in which each sentence begins with the words "I remember."

>how rapturous the experience was.

>wondering how Joe Brainard remembered as much as he did, then thinking that it would have been hard not to once he got started.

>thinking that the "I remember" form could easily get out of hand, could continue *ad infinitum*.

>thinking, too, that the form has an important relation to the structure of memory. That is, memories associatively beget other memories, knitting an invisible quilt of experience.

>noticing a connection between trauma and memory: "I remember jumping off the front porch head first onto the corner of a brick. I remember being able to see nothing but gushing red blood. This is one of the first things I remember. And I have a scar to prove it" (54).

>that Brainard's need to prove the traumatic memory seemed significant, as if the entry into memory—into history—necessarily left some sort of scar upon the self.

>wondering if the "I Remember" form could work for criticism, too: these are the furrows that, after reading, remain in my mind, for whatever reason, after the rest have long since faded and filled.

>feeling that reading is a more forceful process than we let on and that the aggression cuts both ways, against reader and author alike.

>Emily Dickinson's line about how she knew something was poetry if, when she read it, she felt as though the top of her head had been lopped off.

>another traumatic memory of Brainard's involving a "very fat meat packer" who invited himself into Brainard's apartment and, once

inside, "instantly unzipped his blood-stained white pants and pulled out an enormous dick" (11).

reading that passage and locating the source of the trauma in the "blood-stained white pants" and not the "enormous dick," which, on its own, wouldn't have had the same capacity to shock.

realizing that the blood-stained pants are so horrifying because, as the ghastly backdrop for a penis, they evoke the threat of castration.

considering the act of quotation as a form of castration, as a way of making a spectacle of both the severed member and the careful staging of its excision.

Ron Padgett's remark, in the book's afterword, that "I remember . . ." is "one of the few literary forms even non-literary people can use" (175).

wondering what constitutes a "non-literary person."

wondering if any person, literary or not, could write a version of the book as compelling as Brainard's.

in other words, wondering if Brainard's idiosyncrasies brought off the book's magic or if the form itself did. That is, was there something inherently evocative about the act of remembrance or did its interestingness depend on the abilities of the *I*.

Brainard's letter to Anne Waldman about the book: "I am way, way up these days over a piece I am still writing called *I Remember*. I feel very much like God writing the Bible. I mean, I feel like I am not really writing it but that it is because of me that it is being written" (171).

thinking this analogy suggested that profundity was built into the "I remember" form, in the same way that the tenor of the permuting end words in a sestina always creates a distinctive atmosphere, almost irrespective of what the author does with the fronts of the lines.

being struck by the muted centrality of the *I*, by how inconspicuous it made itself by virtue of its pervasiveness.

the shock of recognition when you've done it, too: "I remember running my hand under a restaurant table and feeling all the gum" (26).

thinking that this shock was akin to the sticky, uncomfortable feeling of the gum itself: someone else was here, you shamefully but excitedly realize.

wondering why I was never more disgusted than I was when, as a child, I felt gum under a table. And why I felt under in the first place.

thinking of the book: this is what it means to be human. This vast warehouse of memories is what it looks like in the final analysis.

Brainard's many admissions of embarrassment and awkwardness, particularly sexual embarrassment: "I remember, in the heart of passion once, trying to get a guy's turtle-neck sweater off. But it turned out not to be a turtle-neck sweater" (131).

thinking that queerness, for Brainard, had less to do with the contents of his actions and desires than it did with the way in which he consistently imagined them as irredeemably deviant from the norm.

when I discovered, high on pot in college, that even the people I considered normal, those nettlesome people who seemed to exude normalcy effortlessly, didn't, deep down, actually think of themselves as normal.

positing a relationship between memory and the norm: that the norm doesn't exist but we imagine it does, as we measure, solemnly, our prior actions against whatever impossible standards we've erected.

when Brainard confessed to cheating at solitaire: "I remember cheating at solitaire" (75).

thinking that this confession reveals the way in which individuals are accountable, first and foremost, unto themselves, that social codes do bind us each to the other, and that posterity does evaluate some small portion of our actions and inactions, but that, ultimately, with the exception of an unlucky, famous few, we are each the prime arbiters, the irresolute judge and jury, of our own lives.

thinking that memory is a game of solitaire.

making a further distinction between private memory and public memory—between private and public history—and wondering along what borders the two might be said to touch: in newspapers, in court cases, in books, on blogs, in bars . . .

feeling that my thoughts on cheating at solitaire, whether accurate or inaccurate, "right" or "wrong," were an example of the violence of interpretation: the text as springboard to my own, necessarily differing, ends. Or, if you prefer, the text as the tip of an iceberg whose contours and heft I can only guess at.

Brainard's penchant for zany projects: "I remember collecting cigarette butts from the urns in front of The Museum of Fine Arts in Boston" (14).

considering the book itself as an urgent collection of memory's butt-ends.

loving that the book was a renunciation of plotted autobiogra-phy, of autobiography imbued with novelistic themes and significances.

wondering if I could accomplish something similar in my criticism: in lieu of seamless argumentation, a patchwork tour of noteworthy passages—a reminiscence rather than an interpretation.

thinking that such an approach would bring criticism closer to the practices of reading and teaching literature, at least as I've slowly come to practice them.

going through a phase, now past, where I considered my primary responsibility as a teacher to point, ecstatically, to interesting things more so than to say something pointed about them.

associating, for as long as I can remember, reading and writing with pleasure and excitement, even during times in my life when I didn't read or write much—when I was emphatically a "non-literary person."

becoming aware of the participles, predominantly cognitive ones, this form has forced me to rely upon—wondering, thinking, noticing, feeling, reading, locating, realizing, considering, agreeing, positing, making, loving, associating, wanting, observing, noting, writing, understanding, lopping—and noticing how few of them were pushy or assertive.

thinking that the "I Remember" form does not imbue the memories with heavy-handed meanings.

observing that Brainard's use of the form often functions as an affirmation of the thing he's remembering, its importance as object-event, its solidity within the life of the mind: "I remember zipper notebooks. I remember that girls hugged them to their breasts and that boys carried them loosely at one side" (37).

feeling that the zipper notebooks here are first and foremost a thing, a throbbing fact: a cultural relic Brainard finds fascinating and not a symbol to be deciphered, unpacked, explained.

again, Brainard's need to prove his first memory, to assert that it did in fact happen.

noting another usage of "I remember" in this vein: "I remember how long a seemingly empty tube of toothpaste can go on and on and on" (153).

writing in my notebook that, as used here, "I remember" doesn't mean "I remember an episode from my past": the above remark is a general truism about toothpaste tubes more than it is a specific memory.

finally understanding "I remember" as a rhetorical consecration: this, the following, matters, somehow, to me, perhaps, even, to you.

Brainard's memory of a distant relative's penny collection, how, as a child, the collection appeared to him "almost holy: like a shrine" (116).

considering the act of remembrance, public or private, as a form of enshrinement.

thinking that these observations might explain the *I*'s diffidence: guarding the left-hand margin of the page like a regiment in strict formation, its recurrence serves a ritualistic function and is not a narcissistic assertion of individual importance.

lopping off the words "I remember" from the fronts of these sentences.

thinking that this mass excision was like removing the fatty rim surrounding a piece of meat.

Oulipo

The Exercise and Oulipo

: Context

A mainstay of creative writing curricula for decades, Raymond Queneau's 1947 *Exercises in Style* consists of a series of short stories in which the same inconsequential, two paragraph-long story — in which the narrator crosses paths with a stranger twice in one day — is told in ninety-nine stylistically different ways. Along with François Le Lionnais, Queneau was co-founder of Oulipo.

: What was I trying to do?

"The Exercise and Oulipo" was the first chapter of this book that I wrote, so I was eager to prove to myself, through an exhaustive catalogue of styles and forms, that my project was indeed realizable. In the process, I inadvertently wrote a book in the space of an essay. That I didn't stop here when I very well could have — that I produced nearly seven hundred more pages on the subject — shows that even the most elegant of proofs requires acres of messy computation in the margins, just to make sure you got the math right.

The Exercise and Oulipo

Notation: The notion of the exercise is fundamental to Oulipian writing praxis.

Synonyms: The concept of the workout is foundational to constraint-based compositional practice.

Antonyms: The sensation of idleness is inessential to Surrealistic-speaking caprice.

W+7: The novice of the exordium is furtive to Oulipian xenophobia precipice.

Double Entry: The notion and the concept of the exercise and of training is fundamental and central to Oulipian and constraint-based writing and inscription praxis and practice.

Compound-words: The heavy-duty writing-notion of the exercise-text tune-up is well-nigh the centerpiece of a constraint-based work-out praxis-ethic.

Homeoptotes: The notion of the exertion motion action in reproduction is constitutional to the coercion composition addiction.

Canada Dry: This motion of the exorcism is firmamental to Ou-leapian lightning taxes.

Definitional: The conception or idea of something done or performed as a means of practice or training exists or lives as a basic principle, rule, law, or the like, that serves as a groundwork of a system to Oulipian inscription convention, habit, or custom.

Distinguo: The notion (not to be confused as a concept) of the exercise (as distinct from the workout) is fundamental (and not simply important) to Oulipian (though certainly not to all writers) writing (but not speaking) praxis (as over against theory).

Reductive: All constraint-based writing—indeed, all writing of whatever kind—can be said to be a form of exercise.

Curtailed: The exercise is fundamental to Oulipian writing.

Equation: Oulipian writing praxis = exercise

Terse: Oulipo? Exercise.

Periphrasis: It is with the utmost urgency that I impress upon you that it cannot be stressed enough that this vital concept of the exercise, of which Oulipo are ever so fond and which Raymond Queneau draws out with verve in his lively masterpiece, *Exercises in Style*, is of paramount importance to the playful group of punctilious polymaths, is in fact the governing, ordering principle that lays out and adumbrates both an aesthetic and—just as important—an ethic according to which the group can conduct its austere yet pleasureful literary experiments.

Multiple Choice: The notion of the exercise is:
    a. fundamental to Oulipian writing praxis
    b. firmamental to Oulipian righting practice
    c. firm and mental to Oulipian right-wing brackish
    d. all of the above

Evasive: If you play your cards right, I just might explain to you the connection between the exercise and Oulipo.

Teaser: Stay tuned for next time, where we find out just what the exercise means to Oulipo.

Infomercial: *For just three EASY payments of $9.99 you can have your very own Oulipo Compendium, which will teach you all the secrets to exercising the Oulipo way, but hurry! call within the next ten minutes and as a special bonus to you we'll include Raymond Queneau's indispensable* Exercises in Style, *which provides you with 99 extra exercises that can all be performed in the comfort of your home—that's the* Oulipo Compendium *plus* Exercises in Style, *a sixty-dollar value, all for under thirty dollars! (tax and title fees apply, shipping & handling extra).*

Film trailer: In a world where all writing is a form of exercise, this daring group of writers constructs the labyrinths from which they must escape.

Dust Jacket: In this masterpiece of storytelling, executed with characteristic stylistic verve, Raymond Queneau retells the same mundane tale ninety-nine different times, establishing, in a bold gesture of *anticipatory plagiary*, the paradigm of the exercise that would become so central to Oulipo (Workshop for Potential Literature) thirteen years later.

Word anagram: The fundamental exercise of Oulipian writing praxis is the notion "to."

Anagram: Within intimate expanses, Oulipo finds an exotic trail of noir urge.

Marxist: The notion of writing as a form of exercise is insidious because it posits the sphere of literature as a space of free play apart from any political or ideological concerns. It is for this reason that constraint-based writing has taken hold in North America at the start of the twenty-first century: it perpetuates the belief, so prevalent in capitalist countries today, that the members of the bourgeoisie—the social class with time for game-playing and pleasure-seeking—are innocents who, by attending solely to their own personal affairs, are not culpable for capitalism's atrocities.

New Criticism: The notion of writing as a form of exercise privileges process over product, devaluing, regrettably, the only thing that truly matters, the poem as such.

Pick-up line: Do you know karate? Because your text is really kickin'.

Qualified: It could very well perhaps be the case (assuming, of course, the literary-critical community reaches such a consensus) that this notion, if notion it can be called ("concept" might be more accurate), of writing as a form of exercise, may in fact, for all of its imprecision, nevertheless be the dominant model (the dominant paradigm) for Oulipian (and only Oulipian) writing praxis, assuming we take the term "praxis" in its broadest sense possible and assuming, too, that we understand exercise in figurative terms.

Litote: The notion of the exercise is not inessential to Oulipian writing praxis.

Question: How could you not consider the notion of the exercise fundamental to Oulipo?

Passive: Fundamental to Oulipian writing praxis is the notion of the exercise.

Parts of Speech: Article: the
Substantives: notion, exercise, writing, praxis
Adjectives: fundamental, Oulipian
Verb: to be
Prepositions: of, to

Gertrude Stein: The composition exercise is the composition exercise. By this I mean so simply that anybody knows it that composition is the exercise the movement which makes the continuous present present. Many do not like exercise but if you like it enough it is easy enough to do and so I feel about exercise as I did when I first began to write it must be done and is easy enough to do so why stop doing it.

Parataxis: The exercise and Oulipo and the writing and the praxis.

Lecturer: To consider writing as an exercise is to treat it as an experiment, an essaying, a testing out—not necessarily a finished or polished product. Remember, the word "essay" comes from the French verb "essayer," meaning "to try."

Literary-Historical: Though Queneau and other Oulipians take great pains to distinguish their methods of composition from the aleatory methods of the Surrealists, in particular the latter's use of automatic writing, both methods possess, importantly, a ludic quality to them. The difference in the methods, then, lies less in the supposed chance/constraint divide (a divide that is mostly the product of Oulipian efforts at self-differentiation) and more in their opposing conceptions of literary game playing. For the Surrealists, literature was, famously, in service to the revolution, while Oulipo, on the other hand, is curiously silent about the politics of its writing practices.

Probabilist: Enough monkeys with enough typewriters and the notion of writing as a form of exercise was bound to happen eventually.

Negation: It is not the case that the notion of inspiration is fundamental to Oulipian writing praxis, nor is it the case that the notion of the exercise is not fundamental to it either.

Homovocalism: Devoid of hope, where might the wit turn? Answer: An old ploy: build in a binding rail.

Homoconsonantism: Thin? Tone fat. Hex a raucous sofa node: a man tool too loopy on war to neg a poor axis.

Cultural Studies: The surprising vogue for constraint-based writing in present-day American literary circles must be understood against the backdrop of the country's fitness boom in the 1970s and 1980s. For better or for worse, exercise has become a language nearly all middle-class Americans speak.

Mathematical: {Ou, C-B}, X > P

> in the set of Oulipian and constraint-based writing, exercise is greater than or equal to product

Morning Show Host: Is your **brain** getting enough **exercise**? While everybody knows that regular exercise is essential for a sound body, recent scientific evidence suggests that the brain needs its own special forms of exercise to stay in tip-top shape. Our guests on the show today have over fifty years of experience in the field of avant-garde literature and they're here to show **you** how in as little as *thirty* minutes a day you can increase your brainpower through writing.

Psychoanalytic: The desire to equate writing with physical exercise represents nothing more than a yearning, destined to remain unsatisfied, for the idyllic realm of childhood play.

Paragogue: Them notions, oft themed exercises, isn't fundamentally towards Oulipianish writings, praxist.

Revolutionary: The notion of writing as a form of exercise upends the bourgeois myth of artistic genius, throws civilization itself into arrears.

Corporate: This exercise-based initiative empowers cutting-edge users to optimize efficient methodologies and embrace scalable infrastructures, thus allowing them to utilize compelling experiences to target next-generation relationships in the process of redefining revolutionary niches.

Binary code: 10001111010101110001001100000111101

Postcolonial: At first glance, it would be easy to dismiss constraint-based writing as the idle literary exercises of a privileged, leisured class. Doing so, however, ignores perhaps the most interesting facet of such writing: that the writers, typically white, middle-class men, willingly adopt, in their writing, a subaltern subject-position or something close to it—a position where the writer's / subject's freedoms have been curtailed. What's more, these writers contend that such a situation is, paradoxically, liberating. It must be pointed out, however, that their situation is fundamentally different from that of a true subaltern, since the latter subject-position is by nature involuntary. Even so, this complex power relationship means that every constraint-based text implicitly interrogates, willy-nilly, the very concept of freedom itself.

Snowball: I
do
say,
said
Perec,
verbal
travail
animates
Oulipians'
remarkable
productions
delightfully

Melting Snowball: fundamental
physiology
evidences
Oulipian
writing
tricks
ideas
most
can
ok
!

Formalist: Implicit in the notion of writing as a form of exercise is the idea that the way in which something is said matters just as much, if not more, than what is being said, that the true pleasure of writing lies in the how.

Slow: The. notion. of. the. exercise. is. fundamental. to. Oulipian. writing. praxis.

Colons: The notion: the exercise: the constraint: Oulipian praxis.

Spam:

From:	Subject:	Date:
Ultra.books.mailer@ultrabo ...	Urgent—99 Reasons to Smile	May 28, 19:48

Is your vocabulary not BIG enough? Do you constantly feel like women notice how SMALL your words are? Tired of telling the same old stories in the same old ways?

Here's your chance to do something about it! Literature expert Raymond Queneau reveals all his best kept secrets about how to tell stories with style in his exclusive new book *Exercises in Style*. These exercises will rejuvenate your vocabulary **and** your love life!

All this for only $19.99, a price you can't afford to ignore!

Feminist: Juliana Spahr and Stephanie Young have proposed a Feminist version of Oulipian practices, *f*oulipo, arguing that literary constraint is an androcentric ritual that possesses artistic and institutional legitimacy while '70s-style female performance art gets labeled as passé and narcissistic. What this dichotomy perhaps overlooks, focused as it is on cultural capital, is how, with the notion of the writing exercise, a tantalizing analogy between language and the body underlies Oulipian practice.

List: *Oulipian* Exercises
N+7
Elementary Morality
Lipogram
Palindrome
Mathews' Algorithm
Etc.

Anthropological: When I lived among Oulipo, I was continually struck by their artistic selflessness and their authentic generosity of spirit. Yes, they sign their texts just like other Western authors, but their artistic exercises—the core of the group's production—are not created for reasons of personal gain. They are, instead, public property, gifts bestowed upon like-minded and needy scribes the world over. This potlatch ethic distinguishes the Oulipian tribe from almost all other collectives in the history of Western art.

Deconstruction: An ineluctable contradiction lies at the heart of this metaphor of writing as a form of exercise: script, *écriture*, always signifies corporeal absence, a trace.

French accent: Zee no-shun of zee eggs-err-cease eez ee-sent-shell to zee ooh-lee-po.

Imagist poem: **the exercise**

of the mind
at play upon
the grid

of consequences
permutations

splayed

>   like a thunder-
>   struck
>   tree
>
>   whose visitation
>   the children ride
>   like sacrament

Structuralist: The architectonic structure of *Exercises in Style* is repetition plus variation: the same story repeated in stylistically variant ways. This structure is a grim commentary on the state of Western storytelling in the mid-twentieth century: no meaningful new stories—no meaningful new myths—are possible, only idle stylistic retouchings of the same wearied tales.

Analogy: the exercise : Oulipo : alphabet : language.

Sports talk radio host: Now, now, now hold on a minute. The idea that all writing is just a game is . . . I mean, c'mon, you know me, Mike, you know I've been a fan of avant-garde art since I was a kid: I read all the books, my father took me to all the galleries and the readings, just like I'll take my son when he gets older—heck, I was there at the Berkeley poetry conference in '65, one of the greatest readings you'll ever see—but I cannot, I just cannot, give Oulipo a pass this time. It's gone on long enough. When you are making as much money as these writers are, you cannot turn around and then tell me that it's all just an exercise, that it's all just a silly game. Be fair now. Be fair. It's a business. Bottom line. It's a business.

Silence:

Reader Response Theory: The notion of writing as a form of exercise, and the types of texts such a notion tends to produce (such as Queneau's *100,000,000,000 Poems*), divest the author as the locus of meaning creation and instead encourage a playful interaction between reader and text.

Amazon.com reader review (laudatory):

Eye Opener for All Professions   ★ ★ ★ ★ ★ (five stars)

I see after reading this book how many ways there are to present information in different and interesting ways. Forget my monotonous ways! I have found myself in my engineering profession writing technical presentations with a new awareness of the style of my presentation.

Exercises in Style is fun to read on the bus or at home, and in moments of "writer's block." I read the styles a few at a time, and am constantly amazed at the variety of styles given a simple little story. This book is a "must read" for those looking to expand their creativity with almost no effort.

New Age: Potential is the healing of potentiality, and of us.

Stock quote: OUL   Oulipo, Inc.   19.60   ▲0.12 (0.01%)   3,705,084

Text Message: `r u goin 2 libry 2day 2 xrsize? :)`

Haiku: Five repetitions
        Five repetitions plus two
        Five repetitions

Historicist: While in 2009 America the term "exercise" connotes a physical activity done for the sake of pleasure and self-betterment, in 1947 France the term would most certainly have had militaristic overtones: drilling, marching, nuclear testing—the sound of jackboots in occupied Paris.

Queer Theory: Constraint-based writing queers the very category of literature itself by throwing into relief the normative rules that govern even the simplest and most common of literary conventions.

Word palindrome: Writing exercises restraint wherever restraint exercises writing.

Lipogram in A: The notion of the exercise is key to Oulipo's writing methods.

Lipogram in E: Writing as a form of a workout is paradigmatic to Oulipian praxis.

Lipogram in I: Textual workouts are a fundamental concept of the French, rules-based art group that spawned the Ou-x-po's.

Lipogram in O: The idea that writing can be an exercise is a central tenet held by the French art enterprise that practices rule-based writing.

Lipogram in U: The notion of the exercise is important to the constraint-based French writing collective.

Drill sergeant: Wipe that smile off your face! You call that a lipogram!? Get down on the floor and give me twenty more! *Now!*

Tentative: Well, what I'd like to suggest—and I hope it, uh, doesn't come off as being too, um, bold—what I'd like to suggest is that the exercise seems—in my opinion, anyway—vital to the, uh, Oulipo.

Simile: Oulipians write as if exercise were a harpsichord and rules its taut strings.

Epic Simile: Oulipians write as if exercise were an anchor planted firmly in the depths of each new day, mooring the seasick scribes to the tenuous comforts that only habit, routine, and rules can provide out on the wine dark, horizon-less ocean of literature.

Carnival barker: Step right up, step right up, folks, don't be shy. Ladies and gentlemen, children of all ages, we have here today, for your reading pleasure, one of the most amazing, most spectacular, most death-defying feats of literary showmanship ever attempted. The one and only Raymond Queneau will tell a breathtaking, heart-rending tale, a tale of murder, love, and passion, not once, not twice, but ninety-nine, yes NINETY-NINE, different ways. Gather round, gather round, ladies and gentlemen, the show's about to begin.

Filler: Filler.

Game Theory: The wager Queneau has made is a simple one: that how one tells a story matters infinitely more than the story being told. It is, at bottom, the wager of twentieth-century literature. Whether it pays off or not, the gambit could only have been made in a moral universe ruled by the abstract constellations of demography.

Baroque: This dashing conceit—that all composition is naught but calisthenics—forms the backbone of the Oulipian belletristic ritual.

Epenthesis: Thee notiron oof thee exercircumcise its fundafirmamental too Oulileapian wrighting peraxis.

Amazon.com reader review (critical):

A joke more than a book ★★☆☆☆ (2 stars)

The basic idea is charming, but as I suspected beforehand, it doesn't translate very well into a reading experience. To put it simply, Queneau was wrong when he assumed 99 versions to be "the classic ideal" or something like that. Most of these passages are unreadable, at least all the grammatical exercises.

Having said that, I must admit two things. First, since I don't know French, I had to read a Finnish translation. It's quite clear to me that some of the details must disappear in translation, especially as the Finnish language is not even related to French. (On the other hand, some passages generated specially for the Finnish edition were quite hilarious.)

A more important point is that Queneau can definitely demonstrate the infinite variations in language and storytelling. How many viewpoints can you take on a simple story! The varying description of details was pretty amusing.
In the end, this book is just a joke, even though a clever one. I don't think it has much to do with fictional prose.

Legalese: The exercise is the de facto modus operandi, the sine qua non, of the literary properties of this offshore entity, Oulipo.

Anaphora: To exercise
            To notate
            To write
            To leave somewhere a furrow, a heady trace

News Story: French Writing Group Exercises in Style

New York, NY (AP) — They may not yet be a household name in the US, but Oulipo (a French acronym for "Workshop for Potential Literature"), a group of avant-garde French writers dedicated to utilizing constraints in their writing, are making a big splash on the contemporary American literary scene with their fashionable writing exercises.

D. H. Lawrence: The exercise. Basta! It is French claptrap, through and through. Oulipo is not interested in exercise. Exercise is the free movement of sinew and bone, of muscle, nerve, blood. Not these feeble mind-tricks. Write without the letter e! Compose a sentence that is the same backwards as forwards! Write a plot based on the movements of a chess piece and the secrets of the universe shall be revealed to you! It is only so much hokum. Strokes of the bloated French mind-brain. But the brain doesn't need any more strokes, at present. It has gotten too big from being stroked by sordid rules. Once and for all, let us have an end of thou-shalt-nots. Only then can we know true freedom, true exercise. Only then can we know in the blood.

Telemarketer: Good evening, Mr. Bury. Our research indicates that you, or someone in your household, appreciate avant-garde literature. Would you be interested in — CLICK.

Baseball player: Well, you know, I worked really hard this past off-season, my trainer had me out there every day doing grammar exercises, studying vocabulary flash cards, you know, just getting back to basics, so when I got to spring training, I felt like I was in the best writing shape of my career, and I think that really came through in the quality of my work this year.

Subway ad:

EXERCISES IN STYLE
by *New York Times* best-selling author Raymond Queneau

"A truly original work." —*New York Magazine*
"Queneau possesses amazing grace." —*Entertainment Weekly*
Find out what everyone's talking about!

Fitness trainer: You got this — give me three more, just three more, c'mon, baby — UP, one — UP, two — one more, push it, baby, push it —

Sociological: Just as people have been shown to bond through physical exercise, so too can they bond through mental exercise. In both cases, the group coheres by virtue of a challenging, shared ritual. For Oulipo, the pleasure of writing exercises lies, first and foremost, in the friendships they forge.

Exclamations: The notion! and what a notion it is! of the exercise! imagine! the exercise! is fundamental! absolutely essential! to Oulipian writing! *write* it! praxis!

Resigned: It is impossible to explain adequately the relationship between the exercise and Oulipian writing praxis, so why bother trying?

The N+7 Form

: Context

The N+7 method, invented by Jean Lescure, is perhaps the Oulipian technique most used by non-Oulipians. It consists of replacing each noun in a source text with the seventh one following it in a dictionary. In a strict N+7, therefore, the writer only intervenes in the composition in her choice of source text and of dictionary, thereafter setting in motion an automatic process of substitution. In practice, most writers don't compose by-the-book N+7s but instead devise their own related paradigms of substitution and call them N+7s in tribute. The countless modifications writers have made to the technique suggest that the less propriety a constraint feels — the less its success depends on the novelty of being the first writer to implement it — the more chance it has to become part of the collective writers' toolkit. That few other Oulipian procedures have even come close to the N+7's popular reach should be seen not as an indictment of the Oulipian enterprise but as an indication of its fundamentally recherché nature. When something Oulipian becomes popular, it always happens — ironically, for a group so resolutely anti-chance — as pure accident. Such accidents, happily, are as inevitable as they are unlikely.

: What was I trying to do?

One variation on the N+7 is the Eclipse, a text that includes both an N+7 and the text from which that N+7 is derived (or, if you prefer, an N+7 and an N-7 of that N+7). The nomenclature is curious: an N+7 proper far better resembles an actual eclipse — in which one body dwarfs the light of another—than an Oulipian Eclipse does. What I tried to do in the Eclipse that follows is point out a subtle disconnect between stated Oulipian theory and actual Oulipian practice, not so as to catch the group out (who cares, ultimately, if they occasionally break their own arbitrarily imposed, and largely inconsequential, rules?) but so as to better understand the machinations of their methods. Cards on the table: for all their talk about rules, most Oulipians,

I suspect, have the good sense to recognize the rules' laxity. Always playing by the rules might earn you Brownie points with grammarians and stuffy sartorialists, but in the literature of constraint breaking the rules turns out, thankfully, to be more the rule than the exception.

The N+7 Form

The Metaphysics of the N+7 Form
The Oulipian technique called N+7 delivers a strange promise: syntactic parallelism. What happens, syntactically, in the source text must happen in the nonsense one as well. Every text contains a hidden counterpart, a dormant N+7 twin waiting to be revealed. Often, this twin is sheer gobbledygook, since chance, the principle underlying the N+7 technique, forces unexpected nouns, willy-nilly, upon the new text. Oulipians insist that chance is not involved in the N+7 procedure, but it is undeniable that, when using it, one is at the mercy of the dice's whim: even in an experiment like this, where I am being liberal with the constraint so as to satisfy the exigencies of both texts, I am still subject to the vagaries of the English lexicon. The N+7 technique requires the author in charge of it to harness chance for artistic ends. Doing so demonstrates how syntactic parallelism in separate, different texts nonetheless produces a remarkably similar effect, demonstrates how interchangeable words are along what Roman Jakobson called "the axis of substitution."

The Methodology of the N+7 Fornication
The Oulipian telegram called N+7 delivers a strange property: systematic parity. What happens, systematically, in the south theater must happen in the north one as well. Every theater contains a hidden coup de grâce, a dormant N+7 twitter waiting to be revealed. Often, this twitter is sheer gold, since chaos, the prize underlying the N+7 telegram, forces unexpected nuances, willy-nilly, upon the new theater. Oulipians insist that chaos is not involved in the N+7 production, but it is undeniable that, when using it, one is at the mercy of the dictionary's whip: even in an exploit like this, where I am being liberal with the content so as to satisfy the exorbitance of both theaters, I am still subject to the vanities of the English libido. The N+7 telegram requires the automaton in charge of it to harness chaos for artistic endurableness. Doing so demonstrates how systematic parity in separate, different theaters nonetheless produces a remarkably similar effulgence, demonstrates how interchangeable worths are along what Roman Jakobson called "the Baal of subversion."

Masturbation: A Manifesto

: Context

Asked to explain why he wrote a book about masturbation, Harry Mathews, one of two American members of the Oulipo, responded, simply, "Because it's the universal form of sexual activity, and it's hardly ever been written about." But however universal we understand masturbation to be in the abstract, the immediacy with which readers are dropped into *Singular Pleasures* disarms: in the book's opening vignette, we observe an eleven-year-old Scottish girl, "dressed in a cotton playsuit," ogling "barelegged rugby players" as they "smash into each other" on the television screen. The girl "squat[s] astride a rugby ball," "rocking back and forth at moderate speed" before finally "tilt[ing] the blunt tip of the ball hard against her pubis" as she climaxes. The whole scene just feels transgressive, though not, as you first suspect, because of its barely latent violence, or the girl's tender age, or her idiosyncratic masturbatory implement. The scene feels transgressive, you come to realize, reading further, scene after scene of endlessly inventive self-pleasures, because you are unaccustomed to peeking in on people at such a pitch of solitude and vulnerability.

: What was I trying to do?

I have had, by request, partners masturbate in my presence and I have espied, unbeknownst to them, partners masturbating in presumed privacy and can say with some confidence that the former act, no matter how sincere, can only ever be a performance, an imitation of an act whose quintessence remains intensely private. That is, though I grope, in the following chapter, for a sufficiently autoerotic form, the fact that I intend for the performance to be witnessed means my desired indifference to argument must, of necessity, elude me.

Masturbation: A Manifesto

Frustration: another day at my desk and still no progress on an essay about Harry Mathews' *Singular Pleasures*, a collection of vignettes of people masturbating. What masturbation sometimes feels like: running in place.

~

Understand: this is an essay about *Singular Pleasures* and not writer's block. An essay about masturbation: therefore: an exercise in repetition and self-love, with only minimal regard for its object of desire.

~

Methodology: to approach, through the mandatory use of colons, an agitated state of thought-stimulation, akin to the autoeroticism of *Singular Pleasures* and of constraint-based writing more generally.

~

The colon: I like it and use it often: *here comes the orgasm*, it says: here comes mirth, pith, joy.

~

Genesis 38: 8–9: "Then Judah told Onan to sleep with his brother's wife, to do his duty as the husband's brother and raise up offspring for his brother. But Onan knew that the offspring would not count as his; so whenever he lay with his brother's wife, he spilled his seed on the ground so as not to raise up offspring for his brother. What he did was wicked in the Lord's sight, and the Lord took away his life also."

~

Methodology: to scatter my seed freely, wickedly.

Methodology (after Francis Ponge's *Soap*): to rub myself clean with language: delightful, repetitive language.

~

Euphemisms for male masturbation: beat the meat, choke the chicken, clean the rifle, flog the log, milk the cow, play the organ, polish the bishop, prime the pump, pull the taffy, punch the clown, shuck the corn, slap the salami, spank the monkey, tenderize the tube steak, tickle the pickle, toss the midget, varnish the flagpole, wax the dolphin, wrestle the eel, yank the crank.

~

Euphemisms for female masturbation: beat around the bush, double-click the mouse, pet the cat, polish the pearl, rub the nub.

~

It should be obvious: euphemisms for male masturbation are more common than those for female masturbation.

~

Methodology: to point out the obvious and the familiar: to underscore how masturbation courts purple rhetoric.

~

Georges Perec's succinct blurb of *Singular Pleasures*: "A great ecumenical work."

~

Myths about masturbation: it can cause blindness, madness, baldness, acne, and hair to grow on one's palms. And another, more modern, myth: that it can cure ills.

A doctor on Oprah described masturbation as "self-cultivation": he said that women who were sexually unsatisfied needed to learn how to self-cultivate.

~

Frustration: anodyne, prefab language precludes singularity of experience. cf: the linguistic conventions of porn: "Huge breasted amateur jizzed all over her natural juicy boobs."

~

singular *adj.*   **1** extraordinary; remarkable; exceptional
                2 unusual or strange; odd; different
                3 being the only one of its kind; distinctive; unique
                4 separate; individual

~

As a rule, the popular euphemisms for masturbation are not anodyne: however fatuous, they possess liveliness, spunk.

~

Methodology: to eschew false pieties: to perpetuate the odd and the deviant.

~

Beginning again and again is masturbatory: the gesture creates a pleasant friction, generates its own brisk heat.

~

Repetition is masturbatory: the gesture creates a pleasant friction, generates its own brisk heat.

It should be obvious: colons are rarely necessary. But fun nonetheless: an extravagance.

~

To indulge in the colon: to pamper oneself: to luxuriate in loud grammar.

~

A colon is hefty, ponderous: it builds profundity into the sentence's syntax.

~

A colon: a thunderbolt: majestic, brazen, flashy. *Here comes the orgasm*, it says: here comes mirth, pith, joy.

~

Frustration: ever since reading James Schuyler's *The Morning of the Poem*, a long poem bestrewn with colons, I worry about overusing the colon: in the poem, colon clause nests within colon clause: so much so that each individual clause loses its usual force: what economists call the law of diminishing returns.

~

So far: no diminishment.

~

To masturbate is to say: *I hereby permit myself this space to play safely.*

Methodology: to practice theory as practice: to sport at metaphysics.

~

Oulipo: just as you can add the words "in bed" to every fortune cookie, so too can you add the words "for Oulipo" to each of these entries. For example, instead of simply saying "Methodology," you can say: "Methodology, for Oulipo."

~

Frustration: purposiveness: the yen, even in masturbatory prose, for an argumentative trajectory.

~

Methodology: to practice an art of indirection: to move, as best I can, in slow circles.

~

Eventually, if only by force of repetition, this will become an essay about Harry Mathews' *Singular Pleasures*: an essay about how the book can be seen as an allegory for the nature of constraint-based writing. But first: more foreplay.

~

Foreplay: the belief in the virtues of prolonged tension.

~

I confess to an addiction to the colon: to an addiction to performative prose.

Colons: magisterial, august, heady: a bow in their general direction.

~

Repetition is masturbatory, as is beginning again: they do not, however, create the same type of friction.

~

It should be obvious that if you wait too long to deploy a colon, it loses its thunder: like so.

~

from Singular Pleasures: "After sixty-two years, a highly educated woman of Karachi has retained two passions: masturbation and the singing of Maria Callas. She is now indulging both of them, rolling on six thicknesses of Bakhtiari rug to the strains of a pirated *Fedora*. The music—that voice—do not augment her sexual pleasure: they frustrate and delay it. Sometimes two hours will pass in incompatible ecstasies before they come to a necessary end."

~

Frustration: desire, Mathews suggests, functions as an asymptote: it can never get to where it would like to go.

~

Methodology: to abandon any pretense of arrival: to cultivate an ethos of postponement and avoidance.

~

For it is written: "We hold these truths to be self-evident, that all men are created equal, that they are endowed by their Creator with certain inalienable Rights, that among these are Life, Liberty, and the pursuit of Happiness."

~

Blaise Pascal: "The only good thing for men therefore is to be diverted from thinking of what they are, either by some occupation which takes their mind off it, or by some novel and agreeable passion which keeps them busy, like gambling, hunting, some absorbing show, in short by what is called diversion."

~

Methodology: to make self-pleasure something more than mere self-indulgence: to situate it within a network of meaningful relations.

~

Frustration: Masturbation and Its Discontents (acronym: MAID): a "quasi-subversive organization," concocted by Mathews in *Singular Pleasures*, that "encourages its members to invent obstacles to overcome while masturbating": a mission identical to that of Oulipo with respect to literature.

~

Oulipo: a workshop for the sharing of otherwise solitary pleasures.

~

Frustration: howsoever one tries to redeem it, "masturbatory" remains a pejorative term: it carries with it the taint of isolation: of loneliness.

~

William Carlos Williams: "It is only in isolate flecks that / something / is given off / / No one / to witness / and adjust, no one to drive the car."

Frustration: against my better judgment, I am arriving somewhere: the end must be drawing nigh.

from Singular Pleasures: "A man is masturbating as he contemplates a finely brushed poem by Wang Wei, seated on a straw mat in his garret in Mukden. An 'ascetic sensualist,' he has striven all his life to unite in one moment of revelation the pleasures of poetry and masturbation. On this warm spring morning of his sixtieth year, he senses that the sublime fusion may finally be at hand."

Masturbation: the fantasy that fantasy can be consummation.

Post-Oulipo

Bernadette Mayer's Gratuitous Art

: Context

In the 1970s, Bernadette Mayer compiled, in an Oulipian spirit, a list of nearly a hundred ideas for writing experiments; the list still circulates widely in poetry circles today. The following sequence of poems takes the first eight entries in that list and splices them together, respectively, with excerpts from a treatise on scientific method, a pregnancy handbook, a work of literary criticism (Maggie Nelson's *Women, the New York School, and Other True Abstractions*), and a cookbook written by a television personality. The procedure derives from Mayer's suggestion to "us[e] phrases relating to one subject or idea" in order to "write about another": "For example," she explains, "use science terms to write about childhood," or "philosophic language to describe a shirt."

: What was I trying to do?

To write criticism as though it were poetry and to write poetry as though it were a science experiment — a quadratic equation — a delicious Oulipian recipe —

Bernadette Mayer's Gratuitous Art

Bernadette Mayer's Outline of Scientific Method

1. Pick a word or phrase at random, let mind use the scientific method to explore observations and answer questions. In other words, design an experiment so that changes to one item cause something else to vary in a predictable way.

2. Any useful hypothesis will enable predictions by systematically eliminating the use of certain kinds of words or phrases from a piece of writing.

3. Derange the language of measurement: write a work consisting only of prepositional phrases, or, use a stopwatch to time the fall of an already existing work.

4. When performing an experiment containing unique specimens, let them demand their own form.

5. Eliminate material from a piece of your own writing until it is a facility that provides controlled conditions in which waste management operations can be safely performed.

6. The next step is to consider the statistical assumptions being made in pushing metaphor and simile as far as you can. For example, use the null hypothesis to write about childhood or a logical fallacy to describe a shirt.

7. Take an idea, anything that interests you, or an object, then spend a few days rejecting it outright in order to preserve the integrity of the peer-review process.

8. Scientific process doesn't have an end. It's circular: put pen to paper and don't stop.

Bernadette Mayer's All-in-One Resource for Pregnancy & Childbirth

1. Pick a word or phrase at random, let mind's reactions to a positive pregnancy test range from total denial to unmitigated glee to hyperventilating horror. Don't blame yourself for your emotions—there's no wrong way to react to such big and shocking news.

2. The first part of your prenatal visit will involve answering plenty of questions about systematically eliminating the use of certain kinds of words or phrases from a piece of writing.

3. Derange the language of your own pregnancy calendar: write a work consisting only of prepositional phrases, or, keep a chart of what you've eaten of an already existing work.

4. As your baby develops, let it demand its own form.

5. Eliminate material from a piece of your own writing until it is getting more blood in its outer lips, which may give it a dark, swollen appearance.

6. After you're admitted to the hospital, you may be given a routine blood test to check if you're pushing metaphor and simile as far as you can. For example, use the concept of informed consent to write about childhood or dilation to describe a shirt.

7. Take an idea, anything that interests you, or an object, then spend a few days covered with a warm blanket while your vital signs are being closely monitored.

8. You made it! Your labor is over, you've given birth, and now it's time to return home and put pen to paper and don't stop.

Bernadette Mayer's Gratuitous Art

1. Pick a word or phrase at random, let mind's refusal to be sated by the demarcations of "reality" as defined by others represent the most unapologetic example of "poetry-by-the-yard" produced in the seventies.

2. Of course, the distinction between "writing" and "living" is semantic, or nonsensical, in that writing always gets written by systematically eliminating the use of certain kinds of words or phrases from a piece of writing.

3. Derange the language of a heterosexual marriage with children: write a work consisting only of prepositional phrases, or, elevate the cravings of an already existing work.

4. To take up this invitation [to "refuse to understand what one means"] is to take leave of the writer-as-analysand/reader-as-analyst metaphor that has come to structure so much of the twentieth-century reading experience, and to let it demand its own form.

5. Eliminate material from a piece of your own writing until it is unpaid, uncalled for, unjustifiable, and, in a complex sense of the word, free.

6. Traditionally speaking, poetry is an art of pushing metaphor and simile as far as you can. For example, use a private language to write about childhood or evidence a logorrhea to describe a shirt.

7. Take an idea, anything that interests you, or an object, then spend a few days in the apprehension, however dim, of a world in which words are neither spent nor saved.

8. Work that depends on its larger gestures nearly always includes its failures as well as its successes. For this reason, put pen to paper and don't stop.

Bernadette Mayer's Semi-Homemade Desserts

1. Pick a word or phrase at random, let mind have its cake and eat it too. In today's hectic world, with the constant crunch of jobs, families, and errands, it's all too easy to get caught up in the craziness and forget to savor the sweeter side of life.

2. Always preheat the oven fifteen minutes before putting poetry in to bake. An oven that is too hot or too cold can systematically eliminate the use of certain kinds of words or phrases from a piece of writing.

3. Derange the language of traditional yellow cupcakes: write a work consisting only of prepositional phrases, or, match the icing to the table linens of an already existing work.

4. HELPFUL HINTS, TIPS, and TRICKS: Set the stage for an amorous evening with music that's as smooth as champagne. Relaxing to Sade, Love Deluxe helps you unwind; John Coltrane, Coltrane for Lovers jazzes things up, lets them demand their own form.

5. Eliminate material from a piece of your own writing until it is crisp and golden, ready to serve.

6. Be generous with the caramel—and don't be afraid to let it drip down the sides, pushing metaphor and simile as far as you can.

7. Take an idea, anything that interests you, or an object, then spend a few days eating the cherry off the top of it, drinking the syrup for a nightcap chaser.

8. Entertaining is easy—all it takes is a little know-how and ingenuity. The secret is to keep the basics simple and to put pen to paper and don't stop.

Errata 5uite: 20 Questions

: Context

Joan Retallack's 1993 *Errata Suite* is a book-length poem that superimposes errata slips and borrowed literary and philosophical language upon musical staves to comprise five-line blocks of poetry. Rather than try to mimic the poem's elaborate structure, I adapted a procedure from Retallack's pedagogy, described in *Musicage*: "I have [my students] write on a piece of paper a statement that they believe to be the case—trivial or sublime, it doesn't matter. Then I ask them to write a question on another piece of paper—something they genuinely wish to know. We collect these statements and questions in separate piles and shuffle them up. Two students now read from these randomly ordered piles responsively. The first reads the question at the top of her pile, the second reads the first statement as if it were the answer; and of course it is the answer." The idea for this exercise comes from John Cage's Zen maxim, "All answers are answers to all questions."

: What was I trying to do?

As a sometime professional gambler, I know quite well that there is no such thing as luck, only the immutable law of averages.

Errata 5uite: 20 Questions

All answers are answers to all questions.
— John Cage

Q: Why is it so hard to pose questions to which one doesn't already think one knows the answer?
A: Because consumerism's vice grip on the globe shall only abate when we have picked the dinosaurs' bones clean of their marrow.

Q: When Ludwig Wittgenstein writes that "the limits of my language mean the limits of my world," how am I supposed to know what constitutes my language?
A: It [your language] is at once a subject and a predicate.

Q: Whence ecstasy's impermanence?
A: The Internet has eroded our attention span and there is no going back, only vain, nostalgic efforts at amelioration.

Q: What are the consequences of normative typography?
A: Artistic difficulty can be viewed as a training ground for one's aesthetico-intellectual faculties but at a certain point in the training you must begin to consider wherefores and whys: not as a dismissal of difficulty but as a resolute movement towards one's own groping articulations of the ineffable.

Q: Beyond the obvious analogy to musical notation, what is the significance of *Errata 5uite*'s constraints?
A: An aphorism is a sudden essay.

Q: What are the poetics of errata?
A: Making meaning, Retallack's poetry suggests, is always a process of collaboration, profoundly ethical in its implications.

Q: Why are there always more questions than answers and vice versa?
A: Because although art may indeed be a kind of game, it is not a zero-sum game.

Q: What would "pure methodology purged . . . of the really interesting problems" look like?
A: Word processors are frighteningly amnesiac in that they anticipate—then elide—errors before they even happen. Gone, long gone, is the typewriter's dense palimpsest, in which "apostrophe s restored to pronounce the ritual formula punch in code for teeth (love 's savage splendor)."

Q: How can we begin to account for "geographys loss"?
A: Simplicity is the greatest complexity; silence the loudest noise.

Q: What is the chance a chance procedure works out?
A: Whatever else they do, chance procedures short-circuit all pretenses to mastery.

Q: In what ways does *Errata 5uite* ennoble "abuse[s] of gesture"?
A: Ethics: the study of methodology. Methodology (*meta* + *hodos*): the way the path is known.

Q: How to allow error to work in one's favor?
A: Don't overthink things, for a change.

Q: Why are penetrating questions so much harder to formulate than penetrating answers?
A: Buckminster Fuller once said, "The simplest definition of a structure is just this: it is an inside and an outside."

Q: In what ways is "art a mode of prediction not found in charts & statistics"?
A: The real question is: why are you in such a hurry "to rush to race to wander" in all this "zero sum ergo blather"?

Q: Why, as I type out each of these questions, do I hope that fortune will dictate that its answer will turn out to be, "The world is all that is the case"?
A: Because music is the art form most obsessed with transcendence—with its seeming imminence, and its inevitable, disappointing passing.

Q: How come, even after John Cage, it is so difficult to divest oneself of notions of artistic success or failure?
A: Because the world is all that is the case.

Q: How come the concept of intertextuality is so much less elegant than examples of it?
A: The idea that a work of art can be "interrogated" is, at best, a misnomer, at worst, a form of violence—an "extreme of moving away from intelligence."

Q: From what does poetry derive its "methodological preeminence"?
A: Digressions are the sunshine of life, the very soul of reading.

Q: Whither the arts?
A: The practices of "writing through" and "writing on" are always already collaborations, ways of allowing another voice to possess, temporarily, your own.

Q: How far does poetry shade into philosophy?
A: Above all else, every work of art wagers itself.

Gold Fools and the Question of Narrative

: Context

Gilbert Sorrentino, born in Brooklyn, was not a member of Oulipo but, along with coeval Harry Mathews, is one of the better-known American writers to use constraints throughout a well-regarded oeuvre. His 1999 *Gold Fools* is a 1920s boy's adventure novel rendered entirely in interrogatives. Unlike Padgett Powell's more recent T*he Interrogative Mood*, a series of disjunctive questions labeled a novel, *Gold Fools* attempts to recount a linear narrative. In fact, if you were to change the question marks to periods and eliminate the question words the book would read like an ordinary declarative novel.

: What was I trying to do?

When I was a child, I would sometimes play board games against myself, making moves on behalf of multiple imaginary participants. Whatever the game, the contests were, of necessity, evenly matched and tightly fought: private little epics. I was not an only child, and I did not lack for neighborhood friends, so something about playing a game and not being able to lose must have deeply appealed to me: a sense of dramatic unpredictability without any of its attendant risk. At times, writing this interrogative chapter, I had that same feeling of impunity: confined to questions, no wrong or imprudent answers were possible. But when you cannot, in a sense, lose, you cannot, as I learned in my hermetic chess matches, meaningfully win, either. In its canny embrace of failure, poetry rigs out the conditions that simultaneously grant its freedom and its irrelevance. Let the games begin.

Gold Fools and the Question of Narrative

Where did Gilbert Sorrentino come up with the idea for a novel written entirely in questions? What effect on the narrative do the question marks have? Can we move beyond dust-jacket answers to the question? Does the constraint actually "force the reader to answer the very questions of the narrative itself"? Does the previous question leave any doubt as to what I think is the answer?

Must questions always beg themselves? How many people know the strict philosophical sense of what it means to beg the question? How come those people who do know what it means are always so eager to correct those who don't know? Is it because they have studied philosophy? Are fond of fine distinctions and right reason? If a question begs, does that therefore mean it is poor, impoverished?

To return to the question at hand, what effect do the novel's question marks have? Are they weighty? Jocular? Sly? Do they functions as invitations? Envoys? Koans? Are they as unnecessary—as ugly—as Gertrude Stein feels all questions are? Where does Stein feel this? In her head? Her gut? Her ear?

Is there really anything so tricky about writing exclusively in interrogatives? What do they force a critic to do? What a novelist? Approach a scene differently? Suggest rather than describe? Foreground the assumptions of form? Of narrative?

When we speak about a novelist "approaching" a scene, what exactly do we mean by that? Is that the type of question Ludwig Wittgenstein would have asked? Which Wittgenstein, late or early? How come we speak of two different Wittgensteins? What does that indicate about Wittgenstein? About criticism? About us?

Is it the business of criticism to raise questions or to answer them? Is it necessarily an either-or proposition? Necessarily a business? Would it be more pleasant if it were in fact an either-or proposition? A business?

Can you think of anything so pleasant as disjunction? So rigidly lax in its standards? So unphilosophical, so sneaky and devious? Is it true that disjunction misleads the witness? That it begs the question? That it is a nasty drunk? That it assumes a false identity, goes incognito through customs? That it maintains only the faintest toehold on truth?

That it slaloms through the slender gates of logic? Abets hypotheses? Continues ad infinitum?

Where is Wittgenstein in all this? Where is Sorrentino? What can we say *Gold Fools* is about? And why isn't the title itself in question marks? Does that constitute a clinamen?

What are the boundaries for the application of literary constraint? Does it much matter, so long as we know it is operative somewhere? Must a constraint always announce itself as such lest it be mistaken for something else? Or worse yet, overlooked? Ignored?

Does having knowledge of the constraint enforced in a given text alter our phenomenological experience of that text, much in the way that knowing (or not knowing) there are anchovies in Caesar dressing alters our experience of the salad? If so, does it alter the experience for better or for worse? Does the answer come down to a matter of taste?

Do questions naturally lend themselves to binaries? Do they beg for them? Does criticism lend itself to questions more readily than narrative? Isn't it odd that we speak of criticism or narrative as "lending" themselves to something, as if these inert, abstract entities were up and checking themselves out of the library?

What, though, about the question of Sorrentino's story? Is it precisely a question? That is, does a series of questions produce one giant, cumulative question mark at its end? Or something else? Is it fun to picture what a giant, cumulative question mark would look like? What about a something else? What would that look like? And what effect would it produce? A familiar one? A novel one? In a story comprised entirely of questions, can anything be said to have taken place? Other, that is, than the questioning itself?

Does the answer depend on how we frame the question? For example, if we say, "In a story *expressed* in question form, can anything be said to have taken place?" are we not implicitly assuming that the story pre-exists the questions, that its content is out there somewhere, howsoever elusive it may be? That there is in fact a story and not just the suggestive outline of one? Does the idea of a knowable story comfort the reader? Or is the real story the story of the pesky questions? The way they beg and shimmy?

Would it help further my thesis if I quoted from the text itself here? What, exactly, is my thesis? If I pose my thesis in the form of a question, does that mean I myself don't know what it is? Or that there isn't a thesis? Or that the thesis is about the nature of theses themselves? Or that the thesis is about *Gold Fools* but only insofar as the novel can tell us something about theses?

Can novels tell us something about theses? Don't we often speak as though novels make arguments? Is this a bad way to speak? To think? Can novels make arguments? If so, what do they look like and how do we know they are being made? Do they look like discursive prose? Like an expository essay inserted into the narrative? If that were the answer, wouldn't that put a nice little bow on the problem? And wouldn't that bow—the closing of the question—be disappointing? Even if the problem were in fact solved? Can literary problems ever be solved, though? Or merely addressed? Patched over? Postponed, temporarily, until someone comes along and re-opens the question?

Is there an ethic implicit in these questions? Implicit in form in general? Has this question been asked before? Has it been answered? Solved?

If a novel of interrogatives can be said to talk around a story, can a criticism of interrogatives be said to talk around a thesis, to delimit and encircle it? Isn't the act of delimitation exciting? Much more exciting, no, than the actual thing being delimited? Can we agree that the fence is infinitely more titillating than the field? Than even the horse? Can we agree, too, that the construction "Can we agree" bucks at the limits of the interrogative constraint? Yet even then remains corralled within it?

Isn't there something inherently self-conscious about the act of questioning? Something retiring? Guarded? An avoidance of the absolute? A posture against the grain of surety?

Against what does *Gold Fools* posture? Certitude? Narrative? The cockiness of the declarative sentence?

How can we begin to think about the relationship of narrative to questions? Can a narrative function as a question? A giant, cumulative question mark? A querulous thrust in a certain direction? Perhaps, but does a narrative customarily welcome questions? Isn't the function of narrative to blot out questions, to tell it like it is? Even an experimental narrative?

What, then, does that make *Gold Fools*?

Ideas for an Essay on *the tapeworm foundry*

: Context

A book-length list of book proposals linked together by the portmanteau "andor," Darren Wershler-Henry's *the tapeworm foundry: andor the dangerous prevalence of imagination* is both a recipe book for poets and a critical examination of the recipes we've inherited, an eloquent and absurdist poem on the parasitic nature of all expression and the anxiety of influence.

: What was I trying to do?

The same thing I tried to do in so many chapters: to supplant extended argumentation with a brief argumentative conceit or gesture, to say, in a few pages, what others say in a book, what others don't say in a book.

Ideas for an Essay on *the tapeworm foundry: andor the dangerous prevalence of imagination*

or endings, all fodder for the artistic imagination **andor** a philosophical treatise on usages of the ampersand and the wedge **andor** a natural history of tapeworms **andor** an extended analogy in which the structure and function of *the tapeworm foundry* is likened to that of a conveyor belt **andor** a photo-essay cataloguing Canadian foundries **andor** a psychoanalytical reading of the poem in which Darren Wershler-Henry's past as a gravedigger figures prominently **andor** an unabridged history of parataxis, opening with an epigraph from Charles Olson's *Maximus Poems*, "we who throw down hierarchy" **andor** a personal essay on the joys of having one's cake and eating it too **andor** an academic article with a subtitle so long it puts readers to sleep **andor** an essay in the form of a recipe **andor** a student response paper that resembles a burnt and overcooked stew **andor** a taxonomy, impossibly recondite, of the different types of projects the tapeworm proposes **andor** a manifesto, excessively capitalized, about the impoverishment of the contemporary imagination **andor** a lecture on the tapeworm, followed by a multiple choice exam, failure of which shall go unpunished **andor** an etymology of the word "dangerous" **andor** a rolodex of ideas for an essay about the tapeworm **andor** instructions for a group dance, set to Jackson Mac Low's *The Bluebird Asymmetries* **andor** a defense of conceptual poetry, plagiarized from a conceptual poet **andor** an essay in the form of a tarot card reading **andor** an encyclopedia of encyclopedic poetry **andor** a historiography of Canadian foundries **andor** a book review that resembles an unclothed mannequin **andor** a vertiginously scrupulous close reading of one and only one project idea, such as the proposal to "sandblast the scrawled missives of schizophrenics onto sheets of coloured glass in church windows" **andor** a criticism that can be mass-produced on an assembly line **andor** an inebriate history of avant-garde conceptions of The Author, written under the drug of Michel Foucault **andor** a theory of artistic facture so totalizing and compelling as to be unassailable *andor* leave the page blank, a pure snowflake of an essay *andor* a delirious invocation of William Blake, Walt Whitman, and all other poets who celebrate, condone, or otherwise remain impervious to contradiction *andor* rig out a set of chance procedures and see what fortune dictates *andor* an ecumenical intellectual history of the concept of the imagination *andor* a long poem in heroic couplets whose wit outshines even Pope's *andor* an exhaustive discourse on the concept of exhaustion *andor* an N+7 of *the tapeworm foundry* *andor* a genealogy of the Canadian avant-garde, complete with Venn diagrams and a family tree *andor* a sober academic study that resembles the embossed detailing on the faux-wood paneling in the hallways of the VFW where your AA meetings are held *andor* a work of journalism that resembles a melted and half-eaten ice cream sundae *andor* an experiment in Flarf that comes out even campier than expected *andor* an interview that portrays everyone involved in a charming light *andor* a close reading of a passage supposedly selected because of its representativeness but actually selected with the intention of showcasing the critic at the height of hisorher powers *andor* an unauthoritative list of innovative literary lists *andor* an endless disquisition on infinity *andor* a sly nod to Andy Warhol's Factory *andor* an essay in the form of a table of contents *andor* a vindication of the rights of the imagination *andor* go off on a tangent *andor* a history of the egotistical motives behind artistic attempts at egoless-ness *andor* a procession of encomiums so laudatory even the book's blurber's will blush *andor* a thesis, an antithesis, and a synthesis, you fill in the blanks *andor* a meditation on circularity and the concept of eternal recurrence, in which the universe is argued to be a vast storehouse of beginnings *and*

Cunt-ups: An Exegesis

: Context

A "hermaphroditic salute to William Burroughs and Kathy Acker," Dodie Bellamy's 2001 Cunt-ups enacts a feminist version of the notorious cut-up technique. Bellamy explains in the book's afterword that she has "always considered" the cut-up to be a "male form": "needing the violence of a pair of scissors in order to reach non-linearity." To construct her cunt-ups, Bellamy spliced together chunks of her own writing, often sexual in nature, with a variety of other works, including writing from the journals of serial killer Charles Manson. For my exegesis of *Cunt-ups*, I perform a similar procedure, randomly splicing together pieces of my own interpretive writing with quotes from Bellamy's prose poem, as well as found language from other sources, such as the Wikipedia entry for "cut-up."

: What was I trying to do?

Why, I wonder, do I never quite feel comfortable standing by my writing unless it's in some sense not my own? A cut-up is a lopsided collaboration, a way of writing on, or with, or through, a ghost, or ghosts. If the medium is indeed the message, then the message of so many of these chapters seems to be that I want to be a medium.

Cunt-ups: An Exegesis

Domination is simply the most common method. Brion Gysin introduced the cut-up technique called *Cunt-ups*. I am attempting a criticism of non-avatars. It is a simple technique, designed to produce criticism in art. With a bow to source text or texts in quadrants or some other mastery over *Cunt-ups*, I propose no together at random. Like so many other constraints, the cut-up technique simultaneously delimits and scrambles authors. As Burroughs insists in *The Job*: "It's not, as the author's primary aesthetic function, shifting nothing of automatic writing or unconscious reintegration, like an editor, or a collagist." The conscious nature of the procedure aligns it as a performance.

Traditionally, what's interesting in this context is the demonstration of mastery, as manifested in what the tribe never discusses: the cut-up. Beautiful thing about literature, however: wonders, if they haven't distanced themselves, are attainable. The second we assert control over the **cut-up** and the closely associated **fold-in**, then, is not one of domination, as break the linearity of common literature. They are, Dodie Bellamy's *Cunt-ups* are, a feminist re-technique. In the afterword to her book, she explains *Cut-up* is performed by taking a finish to be a "male form": "needing the violence of a cutting it in pieces with a few or single ways." What is curious, however, is that Bellamy has rearranged into a new text. The rearranging seems to revel in the savage sensuality of cutting innovative new phrases.

A common way is to love smelling it, love smelling your asshole, body. So I commonly supposed, but bedazzlement was aroused: I saw you lying on plastic bags, achieving it. By cutting up my exegeses of sexuality, the constraint is perhaps as strong as intentionality, something it is hard to accomplish in the corpus of constraint-based literature. Her prose, the direction of my audience, I renounce all claims to referents. The parts that feel best to me are my meanings or interpretations. At bottom, this is what's dirty to arousal.

I want to fuck you; I want techniques, literary writing styles that try you until your head shakes like a rattle. A fuck designed to be used with common typewriters, in bed. My cock is normal size, mirror, and intestine. Your cock moves like a wash and fully linear text (printed on paper). Adjust my dirty panties before you lick words on each piece. The resulting pieces are then hot, my clit looked huge, its outer lips sounded of work often. In surprisingly sleep, I strangle you again, this is what I really cut, a sheet in four rectangular sections.

I was under the impression, perhaps mistaken, that sentences, for instance, or Lyn Hejinian's on. Notice the use of the phrase "raw fuck me" as part and whole. Gertrude Stein delineates one of lyrical slippages cut-ups unleash. As here, lots emotional, but paragraphs are and that she mentions of removing skin. Sexual anxiety and / or drinking. Piecemeal as a compliment. Jean Genet, equation of cocks and scars.

Cut-up: a metaphor that violence was a specifically masculine turn in an undergraduate course on the Victorian opposition to "fuck me raw." These are the kinds for which Burroughs' name was enough to rankle, my professor's sentences end *in medias res*. Multiple Burroughs work was rejectementa, unpure, a liberation. Intestines keep coming up. The of of canonical body, and to mention his name, to machine. Cows, a tribute to Stein. The word, the sacred body of literature.

How heartening, chopped up and mangled, lyrically, becomes the knife my father gave me and peels your leaves open. The question of what, exactly, lick the juices from the land of your pussy and any differences of procedure, but in the gap from my legs and there's a landslide along my authorial voice, occupies both male and female. Run my tongue along your scar. My mouth, a sentence: "Maybe my clit could want to do that naked animal." This sack, these hearts bang our mouth, too. The most common clothes know more limbs. A causeway of rock, of themselves, denote gender. The straining and gushing, thinking of you, a thousand violent, aggressive, assertive of control, is a teeth pressed together, you kneeling over textual pieces back together is a glorious wanting.

Enactment of the erotics of violence. But that still contemplates the aesthetic of the piece. These make this a feminist text. The answer lies not in can we establish a satisfying relationship between content. Throughout the book, Bellamy — or the authorial possibility — when she writes that sentences are not subject positions, oftentimes within the same sentence, discovered this by watching her dog Basket drinking completely. And maybe you can put my balls in your essay called "What Remains of a Rembrandt Pronoun Used." Are "you" and "I" an ancient parchment? I want to lick implications — is that the act of cutting? to slice big cookies from reason?

Plasm is exuded — masculine act — then the act of splice, the severed clit, which is responsive to light. I've agreed to a hermaphroditic act, was a submarine, and your pube looked like a little unconscious. At all, it's quite conscious, there's, together with sweat, your tits mounded in a special procedure involved here. His insistence of the cock is to the man a psalm or song.

I'm straining with the subsequent practices of Oulipo. Why years of emotion and you fucking me, you knowing, given Oulipo's interest in combinatorics, that me and I was yours, that, more than anything, my technique as a material enterprise.

One down the toilet. Fragments, the craze for them to William S. Burroughs, who in turn became a century of fragments. Whatever the other nonlinearity and disjunction: cut up, a whole is always less than the sum of its parts. A regular unit of measure, and splice them back, a fragment sometimes implies that, sometimes parataxis. The cut-up technique pieces, divides the indivisible intentionally. It does not, however, eliminate mingled prose, compensating for correctness along the way.

"Slamming" used, as opposed to "cumming." Violent sheets of linear text (with the same inventive descriptions of sexual pleasure). Desire is often a blend of the two themes, somewhat harder for women (they're more secretive, taboo), combining with the other, then reading across isolated, disparate body parts, and not a vocabulary of completed text. Folding it down the descriptions, must pleasure always be transgressive?

Cutting it up into four pieces and rearranging then rearranging them and then typing down, "You are very easy with words, but life is different." Haphazard word breaks by improvising male difference and my vagina. I want to talk so *Fold-in* is the technique of taking two spits on my nipples. You are so fucking, I'll fuck linespacing, cutting each sheet in half. And me like you want to break me in two, and then the resulting page, the resulting text pounded each side of your cunt like a large red cloth across my pussy, like pillows on my skin.

Four pieces is performed by a full page of me. My clit is soft and very pale, my clit so middle horizontally then vertically and cutting loud to me. I'm sitting here and after you fall asleep a new text is formed for your birthday. Can I take violence, lots and lots of violence? Original appropriation of William S. Burroughs's cut-up recurs. Both men and women have nipples, which explains that she has "always considered" the cut-up obsessive.

Our sexual vocabulary is a body of air, of scissors in order to reach non-linearity, of the body in *toto*, skulls. Sex is all about the same technique. Indeed, her cunt-ups, transgressive, stand rent: "I love to cut off your skin as an act in language." Criticism must necessarily hear the boiled skull in your voice when what the critic performs is competence, expertise dismembered. The connection here between unique, original and important insights. The beauty as extreme as it is anywhere else.

In general, we might say, mastery of it is an institution. That several of my students were absolutely the thing eludes our greedy grasp. The performance enthusiasts, I encouraged them, told them the novel, the mere invocation of William S. had come full circle. This, then, is how I always profess.

"But that's not literature," she said . . .

Temple of culture: a clear indication of imminent violation. Burroughs was not legitimate not part overthrown. Dignify it with a middle initial. A violation of Rembrandt, torn into four equal pieces and flushed. When I began teaching at that same, who hasn't written that the twentieth century was filled with absolute Burroughs freaks? I didn't just permit their results and something definitely remains. The story of when I was a student and how the wheel implies relationship to a whole, whereas think of Burroughs as the infection in the something else. The cut-up turns monads into disciplinary gods, mere idols, aching to be.

The Cunning Linguist

: Context

Harryette Mullen's 2004 *Sleeping with the Dictionary* is an abecedarian collection of poems written using sundry, often unnamed, Oulipian procedures. However, the most striking feature of the collection is not that it uses such procedures but the uses — insistently political — to which they are put. For example, "Denigration," the partial subject of the following chapter, operates by means of an insidious aural logic whereby Mullen performs lexical contortions to use as many words as possible that contain the "nig" or "neg" sound. These baleful echoes make otherwise harmless words like "negotiate," or "nugatory," appear irredeemably tainted by their sonic racial associations. Indeed, cumulatively, the poem, and the larger collection, performs a damning enactment of language's inherited — and largely hidden — biases. Working in a literary mode renowned for privileging form at the expense of content, Mullen writes content so bald that all purely formal concerns recede, embarrassed, as trivial, niggling.

: What was I trying to do?

At the time, I was trying, in an unsubtle gesture of profanation, to include as many penis and sex puns as possible in a short spurt of literary criticism, but I can now recognize that whatever extremes of obscenity to which I resort, here and elsewhere, stem in part from content's need to be LOUD if it wants to be heard above the formalist din at literary constraint's mock-ceremonious banquet.

The Cunning Linguist

The diction in Harryette Mullen's "Sleeping with the Dictionary," like the diction of most poems in her eponymous collection, is a bit cockeyed. Puns dictate her word choices, willy-nilly: her ears prick up whenever, by a stroke of luck, an opportunity for one arises. Would it come off as too cocksure to declare that embedded in Mullen's poetic universe is the conception that punning constitutes the whole shebang, "the poet's nocturnal mission"? In many of her poems, it's as though word play were an edict, a mandate for each word's insertion: "Does my niggling concern with trivial matters," she queries, in "Denigration," "negate my ability to negotiate in good faith?" (19). Just as a jazz pianist jerks and throbs at ad-libbed strains, so too does a well-concocted pun warm the cockles of Mullen's heart. But punning, for Mullen, is more than mere poppycock: each verbal poke is, blow-by-blow, a pinprick to our conscience, tipping us off to language's cockamamie echoes. In the case of "Denigration," Mullen's discriminating word designations create an ignitable racial soundscape, while in the case of "Sleeping with the Dictionary," the dictionary, seemingly neuter, gets exposed as a masculine organ. To dicker with the dictionary is to buck at its rigid, ramrod straight definitions, touching off unpredictable correspondences, sticking points. This cocky penetration of sense's jurisdiction, the poem suggests, embodies literary constraint's top chance for making it big. Indeed, it seems no contradiction to tender that the desire to tool around with the dictionary, with multiple dictionaries, is in some climactic sense indicative of the genre's main thrust—a veritable dictum—for addicts, buffs, junkies, and all other members, in whatever shapes and sizes, of the constrained ménage.

Absences, Negations, Voids

: Context

In Doug Nufer's 2004 novel *Negativeland* every sentence contains a form of negation. As the book's title suggests, this constraint creates a fictional world with an atmosphere of pronounced pessimism. Nufer — perhaps the contemporary American writer most committed to literary constraint and certainly one of the most wildly inventive to work in the mode — has a knack, as most accomplished writers do, for allowing his chosen constraints maximum self-reflexivity. Numerous Oulipians have defined self-reflexivity as a necessary ingredient for successful constrained work and it's not hard to see why: recursion calls attention to itself, signals that something strange is afoot. But beyond its attention grabbing properties, recursion possesses pleasing fractal elegance, like looking down a hall of mirrors or watching someone on TV watching someone on TV watching someone on TV. Immanuel Kant defined the sublime not as a property intrinsic to beautiful objects but as the mind's vertiginous awareness of that beauty's magnitude. In this light, Oulipian contrivances resemble little machines for the manufacture of patterned sublimity.

: What was I trying to do?

At the sentential level, my goal was to mimic Nufer's constraint of negation. At the level of the larger essay, I added a constraint on top of that: to analyze *Negativeland*, somewhat tongue-in-cheek, on the basis of what's not included in it. I've always been intrigued by the critical move, Feminist in nature, to analyze a text based on what's missing from it. There are certainly times when such a move feels important and illuminating (why, for example, are there so few female members of the Oulipo?), but all writing leaves out, of necessity, so many different things that cataloguing and analyzing them could continue ad infinitum. Harry Mathews' tenuous claim that "writing works exclusively by what the writer leaves out" served as my provocation: What would happen if you analyzed a text based primarily on what it leaves out? I assumed that a farce of the interpretive act would ensue, but to my surprise the material resisted devolving into farce. I really do mean it when I say that the material itself — its abundant negativity, its looming absences — resisted the devolution. It is easy enough to imagine a critical manhunt for the omitted that deliberately descends into absurdist caricature but somehow negation's gravitational pull kept things straight-faced. Absences, at least conspicuous ones, possess a presence — sober, incandescent — all their own.

Absences, Negations, Voids

> If providing somethings will not do, the writer must provide nothings. I am not playing with words. A little observation will show you that writers do nothing else. They make the experience of consciousness available through nothings—absences, negations, voids. To put it another way, writing works exclusively by what the writer leaves out. — Harry Mathews, "For Prizewinners"

Not to nitpick, but there are a few things Doug Nufer left out of his 2004 novel, *Negativeland*. There aren't any Sherpas in it. Nor are there any ice cream trucks. And for the life of me, I couldn't find one mention of steroids. In a novel where the anti-hero is a former Olympic champion who used to promote Health Spas and who likes to watch baseball games, how could the topic of steroids not come up at least once? For that matter, how could Sherpas and ice cream trucks not? Who doesn't like to eat ice cream off the street or mountaineer in Nepal? An irresponsible critic might overlook these glaring omissions, but not I. In an "environment," like that of *Negativeland*, "rigged for deprivation," nothing is not a clue to meaning (103). In fact, by this logic, what isn't in the novel is far more important than what is, because what is in it is there solely to point to what isn't.

To begin, there's no mention of Oulipo in the novel. Nonetheless, in the book's adoption of constraint, the group's presence can be felt everywhere: no sentence gets included without containing some form of negation. Not an impossible constraint, but an insistent one. Cumulatively, characters and events come to be defined by what they are not, as in this description of the housewife Susan Griffin: "the cut of her clothes wasn't so domestic that a guy didn't want to keep looking at her" (147). Each negation, in addition to asserting that something is not the case, also implicitly asserts Nufer's allegiance to writing under conditions of deprivation and duress. Like an ascetic, he will not permit himself certain liberties and forms of behavior. They are out of bounds, off limits, not for his eyes and ears.

More than any other work of literary constraint, *Negativeland* suggests the Oulipian credo is a negative one, a credo of thou-shalt-nots. I say this descriptively, not pejoratively. A negative credo's neither good nor bad in and of itself. Freedom *from* is not inherently worse than freedom *for*, only different. A constraint always says: *no*. Yet this *no* does not simply demarcate the boundaries of the possible, of the pastures the writer's language has been confined to, but resounds longingly for those things that are forbidden to it, those things that are missing, absent, not here. Non-existence haunts every work of constraint. Ghosts of the unsaid and the unsayable populate their caesuras, silences, malapropisms. The condition is not unlike a phantom limb: an absence that can be felt. No wonder Harry Mathews, an Oulipian, believes that "writing works exclusively by what the writer leaves out." No wonder Georges Perec, Holocaust scion, wrote *La Disparition*, a novel of proscriptive disappearances. No wonder Charles Lamb never mentions his matricidal sister in his otherwise autobiographical *Essays of Elia*. They all know something not everybody does: unlike gains, losses needn't be articulated to become tangible, present, real.

Nowhere in *Negativeland* will you find a discussion of game theory, or even Pascal's wager, but you don't have to be a mathematician or literary critic to recognize that the book theorizes extensively about losses and gains in gambling and in language. The novel's two protagonists, Ken Honochick, a former Olympic gold medalist in the backstroke, and his landlady-turned-girlfriend, Miriam, who used to work in a photo lab developing negatives, are both unemployed and support themselves by gambling as they travel around the United States. This detail is not unimportant: another of Nufer's constrained novels, *Never Again*, is a picaresque journey through the protagonist, *I*'s, various forms of employment—*I* has a surfeit of jobs, while Chick and Miriam have a pronounced lack of them. It could be argued that no theme is more important to Nufer than jobs (then again, the converse could be argued as well). Whatever side of the debate you're on, pro or con, the key point is that Chick and Miriam exist outside an economy of paid labor. Indeed, they consider themselves unfit for even simple household chores: "Even undemanding chores were too much for us. She could say we'd make do, but she had abandoned a building because she hadn't done any maintenance. Usually, things were the other way around, as the pride of ownership kept a place up while tenants didn't flinch to save it from falling down, but a lot of what we did was the other way around" (89).

"A lot of what we did was the other way around": not only is professional gambling an unstable source of income, it is also an unusual one. Its appeal lies in the bewitching alchemy of creating something out of nothing. When you win a bet, no substantial labor has been expended, no goods produced, and yet, voilà, fortune showers you with undeserved riches. A Marxist might even say that the process was capitalism writ small: money making money on itself, with no value added to society. But there's a reason why Marx is never mentioned in the novel: for Chick and Miriam, this modus operandi constitutes the core of a contrarian ethic, a way of opting out, of saying no to the predominant, and stifling, modes of existence.

Within the upside-down logic of the novel, this emphatic no is actually an affirmation. There is no positive thinking in the novel; or, more precisely, there are no positive portrayals of positive thinking. None of the conventional hierarchies or value-systems hold; they have all been inverted. Thus when Chick's former father-in-law Roger Patterson, an unctuous PR man who was the mastermind behind Chick's post-Olympiad promotional tour for the Gold Medal Health Spas, solemnly declares, "What we, what Gold Medal Health Spas is all about, in a nutshell, is life not death ... we are here to help our clients release themselves from the gym-teacher induced inhibitions and retrograde disciplinary mechanisms that thwart self-actualization," his blustery, canned rhetoric makes it apparent that, contrary to what he insists, he actually stands on the side of death, not life (94). His cloying mantras, such as "Language is the audio of image," are not, as he claims, mechanisms for "self-actualization," but a form of death-in-life, of language and thought gone rancid (93). And when he asserts, in response to Chick's protestations, that "Gold Medal Health Spas is not about negative thinking. Hostility is not progress but regression, the enemy of growth," his principal character flaw is revealed to be an incapacity for negative thought: a profound inability to imagine alternative ways of knowing and of thinking, an inability to understand that even hostility and negativity can be means of forward progress, that growth is not an unqualified virtue (96). *Negativeland* never mentions John Keats's concept of negative capability, but if the concept had been included it would not be used to describe Roger Patterson.

Even Chick's and Miriam's gambling wins and losses are perverse, defiant, backwards—not at all what you'd expect them to be. When they play blackjack at a casino they don't aspire to win by being dealt favorable cards but to win by the dealer being dealt unfavorable cards: "We didn't hope for tens and aces for ourselves as much as for the dealer to get stuck with dregs, and often we won by standing below seventeen while the dealer busted himself" (45). In keeping with their contrarian ethic, Chick and Miriam prefer to win by not losing. For them, winning is not its own positive state but simply the absence of loss and thus, in a bizarre reversal, can be considered as a hidden state of loss: the loss of loss. The converse, of course, holds as well — that loss is the absence of gain—but is not nearly as radical a proposition, because loss is understood as a state of absence in the first place. One of the implications of this logic is that the characters become inured to loss, unaffected by it: because loss is everywhere, there's no sense fighting it or even caring much about it. For example, after a not so good session at the horse track, Chick explains, "What I lost didn't bother me as much as what I hadn't won" (20).

Among the many things you won't find in *Negativeland*, the most telling may be its lack of nostalgia for things that are lost, missing, absent, not here. In the same way that Chick and Miriam's negative, gambler's logic inures them to loss, it wouldn't be a stretch to argue that the deliberate use of constraint inures a writer to it as well. A constraint always says: no. But this no is less similar to the delighted squeals of a masochist, writhing in pleasure on the rack, than it is to the yelp of abject terror by a character in a horror film—an expression of surprise mingled with helplessness—who has seen something she'd rather have not. Literary constraint, in other words, isn't fundamentally about being bound and gagged, but about being benumbed, distant, arch. A psychoanalyst might describe this condition as a state of denial, as a refusal to confront someone or something that haunts the writer, but there's a reason why there are no psychoanalysts in the novel: the diagnosis is incorrect. Non-acceptance is a more accurate description of the condition: not a denial of loss's existence, an inability to acknowledge it, but a refusal to be cowed or waylaid by it—a refusal, ultimately, to play games, to make meaning, on terms other than one's own.

These refusals account for the reason why, in a novel jam-packed with negativity, there isn't, as one would expect, an unhappy ending. Two negatives (Chick and Miriam) combine to make a positive (a new, albeit unorthodox, life together). It is not unlike the way in which, philosophically speaking, a proposition that is not *not*-true is in fact the case. In the final scene of the novel, Chick and Miriam attend a New Year's Eve party, uninvited, at the house where Chick grew up in Florida. As drifters, they don't fit in with the "lawyers, accountants, salesmen, doctors, and mid-level media executives" in attendance, those individuals who occupy civilization's approved posts and hew to its prescribed ambits—those individuals, in a word, who play, unquestioningly, by other people's rules. Amid this party full of yesmen, Chick and Miriam dance, contentedly, to the song "Nothing Could Be Finer," as, in the novel's closing sentence, Chick muses on the contrasting pleasures of their mode of existence: "She pulled me to her, and as we danced, I thought of the road they [the hosts] had taken and the road that we had taken, of their house here and of our car outside, and I knew that nothing could [be finer]" (186). In the final analysis, every novel lacks something, but no novel is as comfortable with what it doesn't have as *Negativeland*.

Job Talk

: Context

A bravura feat of constraint, Doug Nufer's 2004 *Never Again*, a 200-page novel written without using any word twice, takes Ezra Pound's imperative to make it new to its lexical extreme. What can be said about such a literary high wire act that hasn't already been said before? Only that no amount of superlatives could exhaust the ravishing complexity of the book's elegantly simple conceit.

: What was I trying to do?

I'd run an unintelligent race, going out much too fast, a pace I knew I couldn't handle, and now, as I gasped through the final mile, I was suffering for my imprudence. The stifling summer heat, rising in waves off the Bronx asphalt, wasn't helping, either. But as I entered Yankee stadium, warning track dirt crunching underfoot, the abdominal cramp I'd had for much of this "Race to Home Plate" disappeared. Or, if it didn't quite disappear, it became an afterthought, something to reckon with, sun parched, after I'd crossed the finish line. For the moment, I was *on the field at Yankee Stadium*. Not playing baseball, sure, but circling the outfield grass, freshly mown, nonetheless. A recent high-school graduate, I was no longer young enough to fantasize myself, as I ran, an actual Yankee — sprinting, perhaps, to snag a deep fly ball — but the proximity to Yankee byways felt bracing. *These steps, retraced, pay tribute*: like my kick around Yankee Stadium, criticism, however critical, always offers its object, quoted and caressed, a similar tithe. That I've chosen to pay mine through mimicry and pastiche means only that I feel, as a critic, particularly indebted to the objects of my admiration.

Job Talk

Never Again's plot: protagonist seeks gainful employment after unforeseen foreclosure strikes. "When the racetrack closed forever," novel begins, "I had to get a job" (3). Gamblers exist beyond traditional societal strictures: families, nine-to-fives, commutes, bosses, salaries, taxes, white picket fences. Citizens—employers—distrust them, consider their unorthodox modus operandi threatening: "References?" poses interviewer, "cocked brow adjusting monocle glinting somber intent" (3). Guileful hero's workaround: craft phony CV.

Outsider status grants unique perspective vis-à-vis ubiquitous occupational claptrap: workplace patois regarded circumspectly. I.e., trade seminar treacle: "Superanglo exec-seminar cant swirls innocent corruptions justifying greed's underlying heartfelt paternalism" (6). Ditto doctrinaire cocktail party patter: "schmooze incorporating jingoistic anticorporate lingo effectively babbles, stymies camaraderie" (12). Nonconformist argot jeopardizes officemate amicability, signifies Nietzschean, anti-herd mindset, menaces corporate hivemind. Moral? Language patterns—conventions—cement labor guild solidarity. Linguistically peripheral individuals resemble orphans, pariahs.

Thesis: workaday world reinforces hegemony via antiseptic linguistic norms, book argues. Jargon's arm extends well past mere careerist strivings, becomes subtle power mechanism permeating civilization's superstructure. Expressed otherwise: commerce's multifarious idioms insidiously pervade public—private—life. Observe evening newsspeak, wherein "visual evisceration counterpoints anchorperson chitchat" (22). Parsed: audience's optical fields, not simply videotaped bodies, suffer disembowelment. Intoned alongside graphic images, humdrum, prim-and-proper newsperson prattle appears dispassionate, apathetic—practically pathological. Perhaps journalistic professionalism precludes compassion; nonetheless, aloofness's naturalization, foregrounded, disturbs.

Nufer's singular sentences antagonize habituated discourse, throw latter's sanctified customs into relief. Beyond providing convenient narrative formula, repetition's proscription constitutes veritable artistic credo: sameness's pert rejection. Technology-driven globalization invariably flattens longstanding regional differences, imposes drab uniformity (upon people, languages, cultures, corporations) wherever capitalism senses impending profits. Compulsively variegated prose flummoxes, paradoxically, contemporary life's omnipresent invisible restraints. Originality's virtue exceeds autotelic, art-for-art's sake rationales. Narrator's neologistic commitment parallels picaresque, post-gambling livelihood. Verbal nomadism's vaunted ethic: resist habit's false comforts.

Cultural Politics, Postmodernism, and White Guys: Femininity as Affect and Effect in Robert Fitterman's *This Window Makes Me Feel*

: Context

This Window Makes Me Feel, Robert Fitterman's 2004 book-length poem, consists of a collection of feelings culled from the Internet. Intended as a response to the terrorist attacks of September 11, 2001 — even though none of its borrowed language speaks directly of that event—the poem is a remarkably poignant snapshot of our collective anxieties and elations (at least as expressed on the Internet). The poem also represents a fascinating challenge to the tradition of lyric poetry — a subjective poem written using only other people's subjectivity — one that evidences Fitterman's ear for the madcap lyricism of Internet pabulum.

: What was I trying to do?

The conceit for this chapter was to appropriate, cento-like, the objective, authoritative language of academic literary criticism in order to write about the appropriated subjective language of Fitterman's poem. To do so, I spliced together individual sentences from dozens of JSTOR articles, substituting, when necessary, author names and textual quotations but otherwise leaving the original sentences unchanged, and then did the same, for my essay's peroration, with several paragraphs from Jane Tompkins' reader-response article "Criticism and Feeling." If the result reads almost as a parody of academic literary criticism, if its appropriated claims sound as generic and interchangeable as horoscope forecasts, if it's ironic that I'm using borrowed impersonal language to make a Frankenstein argument about the importance of personal response to literary experience, I won't claim I didn't know that's what I was doing all along. And yet, again, almost in spite of my farcical intentions, the chapter does, I think, end up making important and legitimate observations about the gender dynamics in Fitterman's poem.

Cultural Politics, Postmodernism, and White Guys: Femininity as Affect and Effect in Robert Fitterman's *This Window Makes Me Feel*

I

There are literary windows before Robert Fitterman's *This Window Makes Me Feel*, including some notable American ones, but his have an unprecedented poetic intensity. These windows are certainly not his only sources of inspiration, but his reactions to them are fundamental to his literary treatment of the dilemma of subjectivity in contemporary American society. They are precisely, this "bird's eye view as I perch on the commander's seat," a new yet old, light yet weighty, crystallization of reality into art (14). In this sense, critics like Helen Vendler and many others who deny that Fitterman is a poet of reality are at least one-half wrong. Marjorie Perloff and Vanessa Place do him more poetic justice.

In this article, I will follow Fitterman's readerly/writerly itinerary in *This Window Makes Me Feel* in order to show how the transformation from censored silence to writerly subjectivity proceeds, and especially, how reading and writing serve throughout the text as the very transformative practices needed to (re)activate subjectivity and (re)mobilize agency. Exploring this interdependence allows us to read Fitterman's text as it reflects a non-unified sense of subjectivity, as critics have previously argued. However, my reading also suggests that while he renounces Authorship, Fitterman nevertheless sees himself and negotiates authority as a conceptual poet.

Moreover, the shifts in the work's narrative point of view—the repeated intrusion of new speaking voices—lead to a similar dynamic between Fitterman and the reader. Just when we think we are getting to know "the real Robert Fitterman," he discards his authorial omniscience and withholds from us central elements of his consciousness. "Intimacy" seems no more possible between Fitterman and the reader than between Fitterman and the poem's speakers: "This window makes me feel like I've always been somebody outside looking in" (7–8). Finally, after conjecturing about what the difference between "authoring" and "writing" might mean to an early twenty-first century white male,[1] I must acknowledge my own position as a "postmodern subject" and experimental poet, and thus, my argument's debt to postmodern ideas about subjectivity and writing.

Subjectivity as a humanist concept has been under assault in the current debates about contemporary "postmodern" culture in the West. Subjectivity is, of course, a word of many meanings, and there are senses of the term that seem more appropriate to the case of Fitterman. For example, *This Window* is one of the most self-reflective, solitary literary creations imaginable; it is always involved with cogitation, introspection, dreaming, and other inwardly directed acts: "This window makes me feel sick because I need to be alone but I can't stand being on my own—my mind is so full of conflicts" (28). If by "subjectivity" we mean the thought processes characteristic of a solitary inner life, such as in the versions of Protestant asceticism associated by Max Weber with an emerging modernity, then Fitterman seems the apotheosis of subjective in that sense.

Similarly, what we have learned from the postmodern critique of the Enlightenment subject is that we should not attribute to consciousness the absolute power to constitute its own world: subjectivity is never "pure" or fully autonomous but inheres in selves that are shaped by cultural discourses and that are always embodied—selves that thus are also gendered. Yet to acknowledge all of this does not mean that we are obliged to proclaim definitively "the death of the subject": "This window," insists Fitterman, "makes me feel alive" (53). It is important for feminist politics (as Linda Alcoff and others have argued) that we remain able to grant a role to individual consciousness and agency, to insist even on a notion of individual responsibility for our actions— "This window makes me feel like I'm the source of the problem and it makes me feel sad and guilty"—but we must do so while also acknowledging the ways in which subjectivity is discursively and socially constructed (18). In particular, we need to be able to account for gender as an aspect of subjectivity, but to do so without either essentializing or dehistoricizing it: "This window makes me feel like I am nothing

---

1 While other writers of the period—particularly Nick Hornby—have addressed the topic of how masculine subjectivity is allied with hierarchy and violence, Fitterman's poem is unique in that it points to the existence of an unexamined feminine reality, whose very recognition alone might provide a different way to conceptualize subjectivity. Thus, Fitterman offers a new perspective on masculine subjectivity as it develops through a variety of relationships with feminine speakers.

but an object, an anonymous female figure to view" (37).

Yet, while Fitterman's project certainly involves a search for a voice or language of his own, he does not, as we shall see, find an already formed subjectivity, but rather produces a gendered subjectivity through the various exercises of reading and writing enacted in the text: "This window makes me feel like I'm out on the range somewhere or hangin' around the corral because I don't get out as much as I would like to, so I read a lot of cowboy poetry" (37). Subjectivity, as feminist critic Sally Robinson has suggested, is not a "being" but a "doing," both product and process at once: "This window makes me feel like I am on my way down ... but I've actually been down this same road before ... ohhh, here's that beautiful tree again" (75).

This Window involves a critical engagement with the multiple narratives and discourses of Fitterman's social context. Authorship in the poem is produced as a struggle, as always negotiated between repetition and resistance, as something formed in the space between writer and reader, speaker and listener. Indeed, it is primarily in the acts of reading and writing, in the various gestures of reading and writing performed in the text, that Fitterman locates the transformation he needs to construct a subjectivity of his own: "This window makes me feel like I am a legitimate writer, and as if the journey is actually going to lead somewhere" (59). It is in this spirit that I have situated Fitterman's piece as a starting point in my discussion of how conceptual poetic literary visions of "the feelings" function in the formulation of a post-September 11 subjectivity.

II

Like any other individual or collective trauma, September 11 has proved to be something of a Rorschach test: the initial responses told us much more about the prejudices and fears of the various commentators and respondents than about the events themselves. What shakes us is the theatricality of tragic events. Before September 11, the images of gender roles that circulated within the media were of casually dressed dot-commers and young professional men and women. After September 11, the images of gender shifted to an emphasis on traditional working-class masculinity and wives holding down the home front. I resist the idea that after September 11, everything has changed and nothing will be the same again. The need to connect cataclysmic moments to our everyday life persists; I'm interested not just in what happened on one day in September but also in how that shock is absorbed into the textures of our ongoing lives.

Can a literature devoted to the subject be societally relevant or is it necessarily limited to an individual's private and trivial concerns? If we approach Fitterman's speakers—and most particularly their psychic wounds—from the perspective of psychoanalytic semiotics rather than myth-ritual criticism, we arrive at some very different observations about them, observations which produce some strikingly different conclusions about their identities and the text they inhabit.

Every strand of argument prominent in *This Window* reveals the difference between logic proper, and the logic of feeling: Fitterman's thinking is continually shaped by shifting emotional pressures of hope, fear, frustration, and love. Having distinguished between logic and psychologic, we can better appreciate Fitterman's strategy for resolving the poem's central philosophical problem: interpreting man's place in the universe so as to satisfy the humanistic sensibility with its demand for a benevolent moral order, and the political intelligence with its developing grasp of relentless mechanistic laws. Fitterman accomplishes this reconciliation, most saliently, by inducing us to share, empathically, the narrator's experience of landscapes charged with emotive meanings and spiritual sustenance: "This window makes me feel like I'm just walking along a river and I'm thinking: *Oh God, if I could express in a phrase what I feel*" (66–7). Analysis of several key sections exposes some rhetorical devices by which this use of a sympathetic consciousness responding to a nature imbued with supernatural resonances, wins provisional assent, even from skeptical readers, to Fitterman's resolution of his era's most painful philosophical-psychological crisis.

Fitterman himself renders this crisis problematic, not only by his consistent pursuit of insights principally represented by sensations, but also by his candid descriptions of the pleasures of thinking and of the vital roles of intuition and emotion in metaphysical discovery: "This window makes me feel like a fake because when I handed in the papers I knew what I'd written was far from good" (41). Hence his thought is continually on a cusp between claims to absolute knowledge, and self-descriptions which seem to undermine them. In combination, these diverse descriptions of the feeling of thinking reveal a poet motivated primarily by the pursuit of pleasures and satisfactions which at times seem almost physical, and continually hesitating between confidence in the opinions resulting from this effort and anxiety about their origins.

Fitterman's discussions of the varieties of feeling which accompany intellectual activity thus serve two main purposes: they provide non-philosophical support for his preference of idealist to empiricist ideas by stigmatizing intellectual conformity, and they distinguish the positive from the negative aspects of his own thinking, justifying the latter in terms of their inseparableness from the former. In both of these projects, Fitterman is describing the patterns of feeling associated with his own reflective and creative activity: "This window makes me feel good about myself to be able to paint because my artwork helps me to show my feelings that I couldn't show before" (8). It might be argued that nearly all poetry, and not just *This Window*, resolves its dramatized conflicts through a logic of feeling, not through logic in the true sense.

The difference between ordinary logic and the logic of feeling becomes clear, for example, when we try to follow the narrator's developing thought on the question of individual immortality. Fitterman's continual quest for a feeling of the sublime, for example, is rationalized as a pursuit of fundamental truths which are beyond human understanding; yet the very impossibility of demonstrating these truths reveals their dependence on Fitterman's will to believe in them, or on his search for a sublime feeling which is essentially a substitute for any form of argument: "This window makes me feel like tiny things are beautiful, that there's humor in the industrial world, and that you can go slightly psycho and that will be even truer" (39). Yet his discussions of the role of sensation and emotion in determining our ideas not only show the importance of feeling to Fitterman's own reflective processes, but also suggest a persistent anxiety about the reliableness of a philosophy so extensively guided by irrational or subjective forces. Such being the problem, in what direction are we to look for a correct assessment of the semantic role of imagination and eventually of feeling?

To be lacking in passion, Fitterman implies in *This Window*, is no less dangerous than to be overcome by the accidental association of passion with meaningless watch-words: "This window makes me feel like I belong, and I am loved, because God wants to be with me" (44). This is precisely the kind of delusion which Facebook encourages: the taking of inward feelings as evidences of divine inspiration. By combining a rogue's biography, a blind — i.e., unread — man's thoughts on religion, and a catechism, Fitterman offers the reader the literary forms most popular with the under-educated both of the city and of the countryside. Perhaps there can be no other ground for belief in such inspiration, but there is equally no way of distinguishing it from insanity. What Fitterman recommends in these passages, therefore, is the grounding of one's beliefs on thought rather than on tradition or feeling: "a post-linguistic turned Kantian position" (46).

III

Our reflections about the cleavage between *This Window*'s manner (an appeal to the feelings) and message (an appeal to reason) obscure what we have been feeling all along as we read—that joy in life can and does exist in the shadow of a sense of life's futility: "This window makes me feel great to think that I started this field from scratch and now look at it" (16). If the reader feels after contact with the piece of writing some of the same feelings that the writer felt, whether he agrees with them or not, communication in its root sense of "union with" has truly taken place. In this century, however, partly in reaction to the sentimentalism of the last, and partly in an effort to prove literary criticism a scientific discipline, the discussion or expression of emotional responses to literature was ruled illegitimate. This is the prickly fact that critics have to deal with if they want to talk about readers as well as texts. But even those critics who have made reader-response their special domain back off from the issue, or approach it gingerly, whip and pistol in hand.

The need for a system to justify one's responses to a literary work vitiates academic criticism. Emotional reactions, whether they occur simultaneously with cognition or a split second after, are the main component of the literary experience. Critics have turned from systematizing the work to systematizing the reader: "This window makes me feel like my time and experience are not important to the education system here" (22). I once was the grader for a course in which the professor made a speech, complete with dramatically appropriate gestures, attacking people who allow themselves, as he put it, to be ravished by a text. I can't imagine to whom he was referring; no one palpitates or gushes about literature anymore. But he was still fighting the battle against what has traditionally been labeled female sensibility, warning students, needlessly, against the ghosts of maudlin and sentiment: "This window makes me feel very insecure about my manhood, what with the pink artwork and the fucking unicorn on the front" (54).

As things stand now, we are both ignorant and dumb. We are ignorant of the tremendous subtlety and complexity of our responses to literature because we have not been trained to focus on their affective dimension. We are dumb in that we lack the skill to articulate in a publicly interesting and intelligible way the nature and structure and varieties of emotional response: "This window makes me feel like maybe I'm not the self-assured, confident person I think I am because I feel like an idiot for not being able to handle this situation" (31). We do not have models for this sort of work — they are yet to be invented — but I can offer some suggestions about where we might turn, in the meantime, for help. To novelists and poets, whose mastery of the language of feeling has enabled them to write about literature with eloquence and discernment — to Henry James, Virginia Woolf, D. H. Lawrence; to the New Journalists like Norman Mailer and Tom Wolfe who have found ways of using private experience in the interpretation of public events; to contemporary writer-critics like Penelope Gilliatt and Joan Didion, whose critical stance is flexible, personal, and experientially based; to Roland Barthes, whose work has made dazzling forays into the phenomenology of reading.

The alternative suggested here is not a new one, though in this age of precision, logic, computer systems, and accountability it may have been forgotten or have lost its credibility. It suggests that before valid thought can take place and certainly before meaningful writing can occur the feelings of the writer must be stimulated to the extent that he is willing and able to make an emotional, sensuous commitment to his task: "This window makes me feel like I've really accomplished something, and I must have touched a lot of hearts with my writing" (44). This is not to suggest that only feelings of love, joy, peace, and brotherhood are worthy stimulators of writing; certainly these feelings but also the less-popular feelings of hate, mistrust, anger, and disgust can emerge in response to any stimulus encountered. It matters far less what the feeling is than that there is feeling.

I like to think that works of literature lead a life of their own, which they receive, in part, from each generation of readers that comes to them. I like to think of them as animals in the wild, half imaginary and half real, which we can never capture or domesticate, try though we may: "This window makes me feel like I will reach total freedom" (51). And in this connection, I like to think of that sentence of Thoreau's, which runs: "We need to witness our own limits transgressed, and some life pasturing freely where we never wander." The freedom from captivity that I imagine as the birthright of great literature should be the opportunity of the reader and the critic. I stress the need to re-introduce feeling into critical discourse because I think it is the only way that readers and critics can begin to appropriate their own experience. To read and write, not as if they were somebody else, or as if they weren't human at all, but as if the fig leaf of objectivity has been removed.

Dies, a Sentence

: Context

Vanessa Place's 2006 *Dies: A Sentence* is a 120-page long war story told in the form of a single run-on sentence, replete with puns, allusions, mixed metaphors, digressions, philosophical speculation, and similes both epic and mundane. This rollicking form, possessed of a heedless forward motion, enacts a poetics of the comma, refusing to come to a full stop lest the text undergo a metaphoric death. Place demonstrates the comma to be a punctuation mark afraid of grammatical cessation and the war story to be a form similarly concerned with staving off imminent expiration.

: What was I trying to do?

Writers constantly try to defy inertia, to make something out of nothing, nothing out of something. The comma, tragic hero, tries to do both at once, knowing full well the impossibility, the foolishness, of suspended animation.

Dies, a Sentence

I had contemplated writing this sentence as a list, the kind that can sprawl *ad infinitum*, a simple colon opening out onto pages of semicolon-divided substrata, but decided against it, in no small part because it wouldn't have been as challenging, and, therefore, as aesthetically satisfying, as doing it without semicolons, which isn't to suggest that aesthetic satisfaction depends on degree of difficulty, as if it were an Olympic sport, like diving or gymnastics, in which the goal is a maximum of contortion in a minimum of space, turning the human body, in the loud pause between dismount and landing, recoil and splash, into a taut, pink blade, frantically knifing the hungry air, no, semicolons would only be a way of nominally adhering to the rule of the source text, Vanessa Place's *Dies: A Sentence*, while avoiding its pitfalls and its pleasures, that the comma, frail hook, must rappel the reader down the craggy length of a 120-page long sentence, replete with war stories, puns, philosophical speculations, digressions, similes both epic and mundane, as well as a healthy dose of mixed metaphors, which extend, by virtue of endless appositives, well past the point where an ordinary metaphor might break, as when "at one such point of weakness, an eagle wheeled and struck, shearing the lower limb of the luckless tree and rendering the earth an open throat, from which triplets came, each three-headed, and each head, three-faced, and each face, variously countenanced, one was three spotted young, bland, bored, and beside oneself, unshorn by history or the future continuous, two was," well, you get the idea, the comma, tender tendril, has been enlisted by Place as a pacing device, a placeholder, if you will, that moves the sentence forward even as it slows it down, what Susan McCabe, in her introduction to the book, calls "the rocking caesura," more or less what a comma always does, that is, creates a borrowed space in which an unlikely thought may briefly blossom, like a dandelion will sometimes struggle upwards, for a season, through a sidewalk crack, in defiance of the concrete slipcase in which we've wrapped the earth, only more so, Place's commas, for, unlike steadier, more circumspect punctuation, the period, the colon, the semicolon, the comma cannot usually bear much weight alone, at most a turn or two of the rhetorical screw, a hasty flourish, like a conductor wielding an emphatic baton, and then the inevitable diminuendo, a disappointing slackness, sputtering momentum, such that all parties to the performance sense the end is nigh, that the show cannot go on much longer, as when a *fête* has begun to fade, the liquor all drunk up, the music lagging and dissonant, but a few determined guests remain, clinging to the dying embers of the evening, not from any drunken enthusiasms, it is long past such a time for that, but from a fear, quiet but palpable, known all too well by the comma, of endings.

Not-Reading Kenneth Goldsmith

: Context

Conceptual poetry is an early twenty-first century literary movement, self-described by practitioner Kenneth Goldsmith as a method of "uncreative writing." In conceptual poetry, appropriation is often used as a means to create new work, with an emphasis on the perspicacity of the underlying concept or conceit rather than the uniqueness of the final product. Along with avant-garde luminaries such as Marcel Duchamp, John Cage, and Jackson Mac Low, Oulipo has been cited by conceptual poets as an important influence on their practice.

: What was I trying to do?

In writing about a set of books without reading them, I was trying to fulfill every writer's impossible fantasy, Conceptual in nature, of getting work done without doing any actual work.

Not-Reading Kenneth Goldsmith

In his 2004 essay "Being Boring," Kenneth Goldsmith deadpans, "You really don't need to read my books to get the idea of what they're like; you just need to know the general concept." This coy sentiment suggests a Conceptual strategy for engaging with Goldsmith's oeuvre: not-reading it. Many annoyed onlookers of the contemporary poetry world already adopt such a strategy, dismissing the books, and the larger conceptual movement, as avant-garde hokum, carnival barker publicity stunts that resemble poetry in name alone. But Goldsmith's notion of not-reading, however provocative, doesn't necessitate a stance of dismissal, and, more importantly, doesn't preclude the possibility of intellectual rigor and seriousness: in lieu of the work of line-by-line reading, the audience performs instead the work of contemplation. If this dismissal of reading's necessity is to work as something other than just posturing and sloganeering, then the books' concepts alone, independent of their contents, should prove of sufficient suggestiveness, complexity, and poetic-historical resonance for fruitful reflection. What follows, then, is an attempt to analyze, chronologically, Goldsmith's literary oeuvre through 2008 without reference to the books' contents, an attempt, I believe, that shows Goldsmith's claim about the superfluity of reading his work is not simply sensational careerist bluster.

Why stop at 2008 and not continue on to Goldsmith's present day output? Because the force of his work depends, ironically enough, on its originality—on its making poetic-historical gestures that haven't yet been made—and 2008 was the year when his gestures became, for me at least, predictable and repetitive, tiresome, not new. The work's mounting repetitiveness certainly contributed to my feelings of fatigue around Goldsmith's oeuvre, but I acknowledge that the arbitrary endpoint I've selected marks the end of a personal phase (after 2008 I stopped following Goldsmith's work as closely as I used to) more than a natural stopping place for this exercise. Consider, then, this arbitrary abandonment of the task at hand from an otherwise interested and sympathetic fellow traveler as the risk inherent in Goldsmith's posture: it countenances, even encourages, intellectual laziness, in a way, I suspect, that will look disturbingly prescient in future. Ultimately, the charge of repetitiveness shouldn't detract from the quite important achievements of Goldsmith's work or the genuine pleasure to be had from reading (as opposed to merely contemplating) it. But it should alert us to the techno-utopic tang of Goldsmith's rhetoric and to the attenuated reading future such rhetoric—blowing, unmistakably, in the same direction as social headwinds—portends.

73 Poems. 1994

Concept: A book of concrete poetry that was also set to music by the avant-garde vocalist Joan La Barbara.

Contemplation: Writing concrete poetry and then collaborating with a vocalist to produce a CD and a book of poems could be construed as a kind of artistic concept or conceit, but Goldsmith's first book isn't, strictly speaking, conceptual in the way of his subsequent books. Simply knowing that the book contains concrete poems and that the CD consists of a vocal collaboration doesn't provide the audience with any clear sense of how the poems look and sound: they must still be read and heard in order to be apprehended. Here we can see one feature necessary for books that needn't be read in order to be understood: the content should be common, familiar, pre-packaged. Of note, too, is the fact that *73 Poems* is Goldsmith's only book of traditionally recognizable poems: as un-poetic-seeming as concrete poetry might appear to the non-initiate, it is, unlike the work Goldsmith would go on to write, nonetheless a historically recognizable category of poem. In order to make the shift into a purer form of Conceptualism, the poem proper—that literary artifact most resistant to conventional ways of writing and of speaking—had to be abandoned—reconceived—as a linguistic vessel.

No. 111.2.7.93–10.20.96. 1997

Concept: A collection of words or phrases that end with the letter "r" or a related sound (known by linguists as the "schwa" sound), gathered over a three-year period of time and organized by syllable count.

Contemplation: Goldsmith sometimes describes himself as a word processor or information manager rather than as a writer. *No. 111*, an arbitrary collection and framing of found language, represents his first concerted effort in this direction. Shoehorning an artist's oeuvre into a tidy narrative trajectory can be misleading, but not in the case of Goldsmith: each new book after the breakthrough of *No. 111* is a gesture designed to fit into a self-sculpted career arc. As for *No. 111* itself, its conceit (collect lots of language, "interesting" or not) initiates Goldsmith's ongoing interest in questions of cultural waste, as well as strategies of information classification. The predicament of how best to navigate and harness linguistic excess has grown in importance in tandem with the Internet's cultural reach, which was only just beginning to become pervasive at the time of *No. 111*'s publication.

Fidget. 2000
Concept: A transcription of every movement Goldsmith's body made during an entire day, recorded on Bloomsday, June 16, 1997.

Contemplation: As Goldsmith himself admits, it isn't possible to notate every movement one's body makes. Our bodies make far more movements than can be recorded by one individual. In *Fidget*, then, a gap opens up between the theoretical ideal of the book's concept and the reality that its concept can never be fully realized. And just as there exists a gap between concept and its realization, so too is there a gap between the human body and its linguistic renditions: even the most exhaustive description possible, one *Fidget* ostensibly attempts, cannot adequately capture the body's varied vitality. That Goldsmith points out, whenever he mentions the book, he had to get drunk in order to endure the project's tedium only points up the way in which a concept inevitably devolves partway into farce in its execution.

Soliloquy. 2001
Concept: A transcription of every word Goldsmith said for a week.

Contemplation: A number of Goldsmith's key breakthroughs and themes converge in *Soliloquy*. First, unlike in *Fidget*, which in being recorded on Bloomsday highlighted the endeavor's singularity, *Soliloquy* was recorded over the course of an ordinary week (though Goldsmith cannily selected a week in which, on day one, he had a lunch meeting with the prominent literary critic Marjorie Perloff). Similar to the way John Cage drew audiences' attention to the world's dense soundscapes,

Goldsmith draws our attention to just how much language we produce (and hear) in the course of our daily lives: roughly five hundred pages' worth per person per week. Refusing to take the trivial and the mundane for granted, *Soliloquy* assays ordinary speech. At the same time that it chronicles ordinariness, the book also represents the apotheosis of a strain of Warholian showmanship and self-promotion in Goldsmith's writing. In *Fidget* and *Soliloquy*, the two works that put Goldsmith on the contemporary poetic map, the subject is not simply the quotidian world, but the quotidian world as experienced by Kenneth Goldsmith, conceptual poet-in-the-making. Recording every word you speak for a week and publishing it as a book is not only a fascinating experiment in autobiography, narrative, and language, but also an act of narcissistic exhibitionism, with the latent potential to create a cult of authorship around the work. In this respect, *Soliloquy* is of a piece with the voyeuristic wing of mass culture — reality television, amateur pornography, documentary style sitcoms, Facebook, Twitter, mass-marketed memoirs — that has as one of its goals, or at least one of its effects, the irresistible alchemy whereby ordinary citizens, broadcast, attain notoriety for no other reason, really, than that they've been broadcast. Indeed, the book's curiously chosen title — presumably, few of Goldsmith's words were uttered as actual soliloquies — can be seen as a gloss on the way in which the soliloquy as a dramatic form speaks to our networked age's confessional mentality: even when we're at our most intimate, talking out loud to ourselves, we like to imagine that there is nonetheless a larger audience for our lucubrations.

Head Citations. 2002
Concept: A collection of over 800 misheard song lyrics.

Contemplation: More so than any other conceptual poet, Goldsmith's oeuvre makes apparent the intimate connection between piracy and collection: stealing, copying, borrowing, and transcribing all stem from a desire to gather and hoard. And hoarding and collecting stem from a desire to create a context for possession: done not for its own sake but as part of a larger series within which each individual unit has greater meaning than it could alone. Music has been the most pirated art form in the digital age and the gathered song lyrics in *Head Citations* are a not-so-distant-cousin of the by-now ubiquitous iPod playlist.

Day. 2003
Concept: A word-for-word transcription of one day's *New York Times*.

Contemplation: Day takes up a theme familiar to Goldsmith's work—the everyday and the quotidian—but marks a transition within his oeuvre to a sustained consideration of the public sphere, often taking the form of reportage. This transition coincides with another: the shift to the wholesale appropriation of the work of others, as opposed to acts of cataloguing and self-recording. One thing that remains constant is the emphasis placed on duration: here, the span of a single day. And, quantity: *Day* weighs in at over 800 pages. Goldsmith's books are like containers for information—or, better yet, like scales. How much heft does this specimen of language possess? That our paper of record, to say nothing of the Internet, is so overstuffed with content means we produce and record history faster than we can digest it. Conceptual poetry responds to this gluttonous information buffet with principled anorexia.

The Weather. 2005
Concept: A transcription of a year's worth of weather reports from an all-news New York radio station.

Contemplation: *The Weather* is the first of three books in what Goldsmith calls his "American Trilogy," the next two being *Traffic* and *Sports*. Strangely, none of these three subjects are uniquely American ones, with the exception perhaps of *Sports*, which is a transcription of a baseball broadcast. Even so, why not call the book *Baseball* if the intent is to emphasize its distinctively American nature? What's most interesting, though, about Goldsmith's classification of his own work is not the question of whether or not it's accurate, but, rather, the fact that he does it at all—and that he does it so extensively. In an interview with the poet Dale Smith, Goldsmith contends that "the critical system is in a shambles" and that therefore it is up to "the poet to frame [his or her] own work," to "articulate and shape the discussion about our work ourselves." Given that Goldsmith's oeuvre takes discursive overproduction—or, more precisely, the feeling that the Internet makes it even harder than in the past to negotiate the discursive overproduction that has always, at all times, existed in the world—as its conceptual starting point, it seems specious, even disingenuous, to claim that critical conversations wouldn't take place without the poets themselves to ferry along those conversations. Critics are producing as much unread language as civilians, if not more. What they're not doing, however, if left entirely in control of the discourse, is promoting poets with the same efficacy and zeal as the best self-promoters can muster. Acting as author and critic-promoter of his own work — an inevitability, probably, for a conceptual poet, and even for most non-conceptual poets nowadays — it's remarkable the extent to which Goldsmith has been able to establish the terms under which his work gets discussed by others, this present essay no exception. In fact, it wouldn't be a stretch — nor would it be original, either — to suggest that Goldsmith's most successful artistic creation has been that of his poetic identity: a Conceptual triumph if ever there was one.

Traffic. 2007
Concept: A transcription of one's day worth of traffic reports from an all-news New York radio station.

Contemplation: In the vernacular, the word "traffic" is used to refer, quite specifically, to the presence or absence of vehicular congestion. At its core, though, the word refers to any kind of movement or commerce, to objects coming and going: cars, yes, but also money, goods, and ideas. Goldsmith's books from this period traffic in the language of traffic, in language addressed to the consumer, hopeful of moving her this way or that. One wonders, contemplating this logjam of commercial discourse, whether space exists on the airwaves for other kinds of language. Goldsmith's bleak answer: no, or, at best, in pockets of (as yet) un-co-opted obscurity so tiny and inconsequential as to be effectively invisible.

Sports. 2008
Concept: A transcription of the longest recorded nine-inning baseball game in history, a five-hour 2006 game between the Boston Red Sox and the New York Yankees.

Contemplation: It's hard to write with finality about the career of a relatively young, living artist, but it's also hard not to feel that in rounding off his "American Trilogy" with *Sports*, Goldsmith went about as far as he could go in a certain direction. Each new installment of the trilogy underscores the whole's methodological sameness: the Conceptual gesture remains the same even as the topic changes. Other books have followed—an anthology, a collection of essays, a new work of Conceptualism—but the basic appropriative gesture, like all avant-garde gestures, derives much of its considerable force from its newness. Its replication, no matter how compelling in its own right, will always stand dimmed—sometimes slightly, sometimes entirely—by the original.

Love Letter to CAConrad

: Context

CAConrad's (soma)tic poetry exercises consist of two parts: first, a detailed set of instructions — themselves of poem-like intensity — for the poet to follow, typically involving a series of bodily movements or activities; second, the poems produced by these instructions. The exercises are designed to enact how "experience outside norms force disequilibrium." For my chapter on Conrad, I designed a (soma)tic for myself that was an amalgam of several of his own (soma)tics, then wrote a letter to him based on the notes I took during the exercise.

: What was I trying to do?

To estrange my habits of reading and writing — To thank Conrad for his own example — To enact an erotics, rather than a hermeneutics, of art —

Love Letter to CAConrad

Fort Tryon Park, Manhattan
May 17 2010
2:45 p.m.

Dear Conrad,

I come to this park to estrange my habits of reading and writing and soon find myself in crisis: I have to pee really badly. Deep in the park, no bathroom forthcoming, I find a tree in a small clearing that, judging by its considerable litter, is a drinking nook for local teens. I make no apologies for urinating outside our sewage system.

In the introductory notes to your (soma)tic poetry exercises, you hypothesize, disturbingly, that "if I am an extension of this world then I am an extension of garbage, shit, pesticides, bombed and smoldering cities, microchips, cyber, astral and biological pollution." Surveying this drinking spot, I am reminded of your hypothesis and revolted at my complicity in this filth: beer cans, plastic bottles, a begrimed baseball cap, empty canisters of baby wipes, plastic bags, glass bottles, newspapers, and condom wrappers, dozen and dozens of condom wrappers. In these spattered remains, I recognize my species — myself — all too well.

Whenever I write, I go to the bathroom more often than usual. I had assumed this habit to be a nervous tic (fear of continuing to write), but today, doing this exercise, recognize it as a strategy for maintaining equilibrium: bodily states, remarkably precarious and perceptive, create the conditions for consciousness and thought. Habits, what your (soma)tics interrupt, are necessities about which we've forgotten that fact.

Moving away from the drinking nook, I approach a rusty, chain-link fence that marks the boundary between the park and the neighborhood, Washington Heights, that lies downhill. Careful to avoid the poison ivy underfoot, I climb through an opening in the fence, thinking that this liminal space—where I can hear, but not see, people on the street below—seems the perfect place to meditate on your poems: an unseen wilderness in the belly of culture.

"Take account," you enjoin in one of your prompts, "of how many times you're not saying or doing EXACTLY what you want to say or do in a day." It may be cliché to say that poetry doesn't like walls, that it's a medium for transgressions and reconnaissance raids, but I don't think it's possible to overemphasize just how bold are your own poetic departures. The bravery—genuine bravery—they require must be the reason why others react to your work with such strong adulation or animosity.

An interesting tension: your (soma)tics use strict, detailed procedures in order to blow apart unwritten rules of poetry and of the everyday. We normally think of rules as limitations or prohibitions, but yours function the opposite way, as instructions to help us step outside our ingrained orbits. Always, your exercises demand something EXTREME of the poet, which is why I suspect you capitalize liberally: a reminder to rim discomfort wherever possible, to "LOSE AND WASTE NO MORE TIME POET!" Sloughing off shame, your exercises take it as axiomatic that we cannot know a limit until it has been crossed.

Seated on a rock, I decide to read some poems out loud, beginning with "Emily Dickinson Came to Earth and Then She Left," one of my favorites:

> your sweaty party dress and my sweaty party dress lasted a few minutes until the tomato was gone some day they will disambiguate you but not while I'm around our species won Emily we won it feels so good to be winning the flame of victory pass it around it never goes out dinosaurs ruled Massachusetts dinosaurs fucking and laying eggs in Amherst Boston Mount Holyoke then you appeared high priestess pulling it out of the goddamned garden with both hands you Emily remembered the first time comprehending a struck match can spread a flame it feels good to win this fair and square protest my assessment all you want but not needing to dream is like not needing to see the world awaken to itself indestructible epiphanies consume the path and just because you're hav-

ing fun doesn't mean you're not going to die recrimination is the fruit to defy with unexpected appetite I will be your outsider if that's how you need me electric company's stupid threatening letters cannot affect a poet who has faced death

Reading the poem aloud while alone in the woods feels unexpectedly absurd, weightless, as if the words my puny voice intone lack a necessary human context or scale. This weightlessness excites me, as does the poem itself: in them, I recognize the passage of ghosts: yours, Dickinson's, Spicer's, Lorca's, Whitman's: all those crazy pilgrims whose carols still vibrate in the ether.

Conrad, I do not want to disambiguate you, your words, I chant them again, they move thick upon one another, they press, ripely, at the edges of sound and sense, pregnant with unbroken momentum, the phrases stretched into one another like the lineage of poets throughout the besotted centuries. Conrad, I want to practice literary criticism as an unabashed love letter, I want to wonder, with you, "how to love/ this world without/ sounding silly," then to sigh, contented, "ah, too late."

With my back to the apartment buildings below, a relic of my prudishness, I begin, slowly, to touch myself over my pants. I am not thinking of you or your poems, exactly, but of being outside, of fucking in plain air, of the ghosts of those teens whose nearby pleasures are only ever affirmed as furtive. When it hits the earth at my feet, my cum does not seem as inconsequential as my recited words did earlier. Thick and viscous, it looks like strands of Elmer's glue.

In the instructions for "Touch Yourself for Art," you recommend bringing a pair of binoculars to a museum to better observe a favorite artwork. I love to picture you, owl-eyed, staring in rapt attention at a Rothko. Like you, I prefer my artistic enthusiasms UP CLOSE, vision exaggeratedly enhanced, as little critical distance as possible. Extreme.

As I trudge back up the hill toward the main part of the park, I think about how the French call the orgasm *la petite mort*, the little death, and about your own fixation with death in the (soma)tics, wondering if there's another, darker side to love: not hate, but oblivion, the quietus on the far side of creative ferment.

Emerging from a secluded, wooded trail onto a wide, paved path, I exchange friendly nods with an Hispanic man. As we pass, he remarks, with evident contentment, "Beautiful day today." "It's perfect," I say, and I mean it.

Back in the main part of the park, I look for an appropriate lawn to lie down on: not the one with two couples on it, overlooking the Hudson, and not the one palpable with frantic children, reminders both of vitality's obliviousness to death. Here it is: a quiet triangle of grass between the park drive, a footpath, and a small stone wall. I remove my bag, lay down in the grass, and slowly close my eyes.

Death is the indifference of noise, I write when I eventually sit up. Stillness: all these bodies packed in the ground and the birds continue to chirp. By definition, an absence cannot know it is absent, unless, of course, it is a poem.

>Thank you, immensely, for yours—
>Lou

Interview with Ammiel Alcalay

: Context

At the time of this interview, Ammiel Alcalay, poet, translator, critic, and professor of English at the CUNY Graduate Center, had recently launched *Lost and Found: The CUNY Poetics Document Initiative*. The initiative was an outgrowth of his teaching at the university, providing a space for students and scholars to perform archival research on the extra-poetic work — correspondence, journals, critical prose, novels, transcripts of talks — of the New American Poets.

: What was I trying to do?

I was interested in interviewing Ammiel about *Lost and Found* as part of this project — even though the topic doesn't, on the surface, seem to fit into the aesthetic lineage of constraint — because I wanted to entertain comparisons between the kind of information management scholarship undertakes with the kind of information management conceptual poets perform. I was also interested in treating the interview form itself as just such a form of information management — and, by extension, as a critical tool in its own right. We never quite got around to talking about conceptual poetry, but our discussions of scholarship made the interview germane to my concerns nonetheless.

Interview with Ammiel Alcalay

CUNY Graduate Center
August 27 2010
4:01 p.m.

LOUIS BURY: Can you talk about the origins of *Lost and Found: The CUNY Poetics Document Initiative*?

AMMIEL ALCALAY: They're multiple. I've been thinking about doing something like this for many years. It comes out of a long history of thinking about why things are out of print. Gilbert Sorrentino emphasized this when I studied with him: "All these great writers are out of print? Why is that?" John O'Brien started Dalkey Archive Press in correspondence with Gil and the idea was to reprint important books that for various reasons were no longer available. I've also always had in mind doing something like Donald Allen's "Writing" series, which was so useful.

LB: What was Allen's "Writing" series?

AA: They ranged from pamphlets to books and I think there were seventy or eighty in the end. A lot of them were so-called "extra-poetic" work but they contained very important material. In the first group was Charles Olson's "Proprioception" and "A Bibliography on America for Ed Dorn," Ed Dorn's interviews, Philip Whalen's interviews. I found something like that lacking in the contemporary poetry landscape.

LB: *Lost and Found* also has roots in your teaching. Can you talk about those origins?

AA: At the CUNY Graduate Center, where I teach, we were facing a local problem of students who work hard teaching in the CUNY system but as a result don't have time to do extensive research and scholarship. As a way to incorporate that kind of work into class, I started a course called "Contexts of Twentieth Century American Poetry," which was focused on textual scholarship and issues of poetic transmission. The class came on the heels of several years of telephone book-like "Collected Poems" that had been coming out—Ted Berrigan, Barbara Guest, and others—which I felt dissatisfaction with. The volumes were nice to have but very context-less. And I found when I brought in the original books to class that students would have a different experience of the poems. Without fetishizing the book as such, there is something important to how you get the poems, what form you receive them in. So my idea was to have a course where students would come out with a publishable project.

LB: I'm curious about the questions of access and circulation that you've brought up. You mentioned, for example, Allen's "Writing" series, which is no longer in print and therefore harder to find, more obscure. What do you see as the politics of textual access, the politics of what remains in print and what doesn't?

AA: There's so many levels to this. In my own experience, I did a lot of translation during the war in ex-Yugoslavia. One of the books I translated was *The Tenth Circle of Hell*, by the Bosnian poet Rezak Hukanović, who was held in a Serb camp. When I first translated it in 1994, I tried to sell it and nobody was interested in it. Then the massacre at Srebrenica happened and all of sudden my phone was jumping off the hook. And I said, "But this book has nothing to do with Srebrenica." But now there was interest in this sort of thing. So I published it, it received prominent reviews in places like the *Washington Post* and the *New York Times*, and within a year and a half it had gone out of print. On the other hand, in 1998 I published Semezdin Mehmedinović's *Sarajevo Blues* with City Lights, which has stayed in print and gone through three or four printings by now. The reason why it was important to publish that book at a place like City Lights is that it presents a challenge to American writers who would look for innovative writing in presses like that. Whereas *The Tenth Circle* didn't have enough traction to become a commodity, so it disappeared despite its initial blitz, which was tied into the idea that we're in the middle of a war and this is therefore something you need to know about. The same thing has happened with Arab writing in the past five or six years. I've been championing Arab writing for the past twenty-plus years, but it's only since September eleventh that Americans now have the idea that they need this material. It's totally indiscriminate.

LB: Publishing something because it's topical is a form of planned amnesia. The news cycle works the same way.

AA: I think the politics of the introduction to *The Tenth Circle of Hell* plays into this as well. I thought it would be important to get somebody for the introduction that, insofar as it would be possible in this country, fifty percent of high school kids would recognize the name, so that the book could go across certain boundaries. My first thought was Toni Morrison—that that would be an interesting and odd pairing. A couple of people flipped out, said it couldn't be done, and Elie Wiesel ended up as the choice, which to me was revolting because he was basically cleaning his conscience for not having initially responded to the situation and here he was given an opportunity to be politically correct. So much of what happens in commercial publishing, particularly regarding foreign things, has to do with the cleansing of reputations, but people aren't aware of it.

LB: And that's partly, too, a matter—or a lack—of context, of unfamiliarity with the places where the books are coming from.

AA: Yeah. At a certain point, I found myself increasingly removed from commercial translation projects because I knew too much and was a pain in the ass. I was involved with certain projects that were literally putting people in danger. For example, I co-translated the work of a former Syrian political prisoner and there was an organization that wanted to showcase his work in the context of the "Axis of Evil" thing with Syria and North Korea. And I said, "You can't do this to this guy because it will get imputed to him and he'll get killed." So part of *Lost and Found* has to do with ethics. Even in the hands-on training of certain skills: How do you consider an archive? What's the process of choice involved? What happens when you have to deal with family members? It can get very complex.

LB: I think the assumption when you're doing scholarly work is that you're working with inanimate things—things that are dead, in the past—and putting them under the electron microscope. But it's not just the authors' relatives who are still living, it's the work itself—and that also implies an ethic.

AA: Part of what I wanted to see happen with *Lost and Found* pertains to the consumer model of experience, which we're inundated by on every level.

LB: It's our default setting.

AA: Yeah, it's everywhere. I'm fifty-four and happen to have had a particular background. My father was a painter. Growing up, it was just normal for me to have all these poets and artists around. They were family friends. It's weird because there's a paradox now. On the one hand, there's very open access: you can email a writer you like, if you're a young person, and maybe they'll respond. Whereas when I was growing up, this kind of culture was weirdly underground. But on the other hand there was a different kind of recognition then. I remember when I was thirteen, in 1969, in Boston, when Kerouac died. It was a local event and a big deal. It's very difficult—without getting nostalgic—to say what constitutes differences in experiences. But what became evident as *Lost and Found* developed was that the interactions with the poets' surviving family was important and instructive for both the students and the family. Claudia Moreno Pisano, for example, was dealing personally with Amiri Baraka and Jennifer Dunbar Dorn, Ed Dorn's widow, and had to deal with the touchy issue of how they were going to feel about the personal matters that were being discussed in the letters she was publishing. Stefania Heim got in touch with Muriel Rukeyser's son, Bill, to get publishing permission and Bill responded by coming from California to a NeMLA conference—where some of our students had organized a panel on Rukeyser—and giving the students old publications of hers. That's similar to the kind of first-hand transmission that I grew up around, which I feel is not manufactured. It's surprising, you're not expecting it, you don't quite know what's going to happen. It's a risk. It's not a context where you're sure of what's going to happen. That's an important aspect of the whole training.

LB: I like how you're describing the ability to negotiate interpersonal relationships as an aspect of scholarly training.

AA: Totally. How do you deals with the archivists? You have all levels of bureaucracy and strangeness, of openness and closedness.

LB: First-hand transmission is obviously important both to your methodology in *Lost and Found* and to the poets who are the focus of the series. Can you talk about first-hand transmission in the specific context of what gets called New American Poetry? More generally, how do you view the historical import of New American Poetry?

AA: *The New American Poetry* presented work that had been circulating at an underground level for ten or fifteen years, which all of sudden you could get it in one place. There are people who disagreed with the way Don Allen classified things in the anthology, but he was working in a model that was very successful. To me, that period in American poetry—roughly 1950–1975—I think we're looking at it all wrong. I'll take the Tang Dynasty, I'll take the Abbasid, I'll take the Elizabethan, I'll take the Romantics—this period is right there in terms of any adjective you want to give to tremendous cultural production.

LB: You said we're looking at the period wrong. How do you think it's typically viewed? And what would be some alternative ways of viewing it?

AA: When Robert Creeley died, the obituary in the *New York Times* was a classic American PSYOP: get 'em coming and going, so they don't know where they are. Don't be too positive and don't be too negative. The second paragraph said that Creeley had mastered the vernacular, which is like saying Langston Hughes has natural rhythm. And then there was a quote from John Simon—mainly an art critic—who elsewhere has said of Creeley that his poems are short but not short enough. Now imagine an obituary which said that Creeley worked in the tradition of Thoreau, Emerson, Dickinson, and Melville, and that along with Charles Olson, he was one of the coiners of the term "postmodernism." Had that obituary been written, we'd be living in another country. What I'm saying is I think we're not close to wrapping our heads around a heroic age. These were people who were up against unbelievable odds, a handful of people who through messiness, courage, and imagination took on a very complicated shift in the total society, all the Cold War stuff, covert operations, a squeezing of experience, perpetual war—things that poets like Rukeyser and Robert Duncan were prescient about. There's a colonization of the past that takes place. The New American Poets are viewed as individuals who are "problematic" because we've now "gone beyond" them: they're patriarchal, messy, etc. All the kinds of categories you can easily debunk people with.

LB: They become a kind of stepping stone to what's *now*—and we've surpassed them.

AA: Yeah. That's one prevalent dismissal: "We're tired of hearing about them." Another prevalent dismissal is this really odd thing in this country, which is that you have this bloc of what Eliot Weinberger very intelligently called "official verse culture," to whom the New Americans are nonentities, meaningless. Official verse culture is what our literate culture thinks of when they think of—*if* they think of—poetry in the last century. Poets like John Wieners are unknown.

LB: What you're saying reminds me of how Muriel Rukeyser writes in *Willard Gibbs* that, "If we are free people, we are also in a sense free to choose our past, at every moment to choose the tradition we will bring to the future." In other words, one's cultural heritage must be actively selected, fought for as a matter of value. This notion is obviously crucial to what you're doing with *Lost and Found*, but I think Rukeyser's formulation of it emphasizes how this kind of recuperative work isn't simply a matter of bickering over reputations but has profound implications for the present and the future.

AA: That's definitely the idea. I'd say two things. First, during the time of the New Americans, the university system in the US expanded exponentially and disciplinarity became increasingly defined by private vocabularies and terminologies. The technocratic nature of expertise became multiplied. There was little place for actual thought. Within this environment, it was often poets who were doing the thinking. To me, Olson is one of the most important thinkers of the twentieth century. He was dealing with the human universe in an experimental way that has enormous implications still. People completely unaware of him are now doing history as he would have prescribed it. It's taken that long to filter through. There's a school of thought that dismisses Olson's archaeological work in the Yucatan as imperialist plundering. There may be some iota of truth to that, but there's the fact of curiosity, of human solidarity, of the idea that we need to risk something in order to find something else out, something that may not be "yours." And such a view totally ignores what Olson actually did: he refused to participate in either a political or an academic career, both hard-won paths for a working class child of immigrants, which he was.

LB: It's like critiquing an abolitionist in 1830s America for not living up to the ethical standards of today.

AA: Yeah, I think it's a pervasive phenomenon, where we see this real colonialist subjugation of the past and privileging of our advantages in the present. It runs through so much thinking. As much work has been done on the so-called New Americans, the surface has barely been scratched. There's lots of unpublished, unknown, unexplored, unexamined work. Josh Schneiderman made a great off-hand comment while working on the Kenneth Koch and Frank O'Hara correspondence, saying, "Why do they call them the 'New York school'? They're never in New York together." And throughout *Lost and Found*—with the exception of the work on Rukeyser, who precedes the other poets by a bit—all the poets in the First Series, for instance, are mentioned elsewhere in the series. In the Koch-O'Hara correspondence you'll see references to Creeley, Whalen, Baraka. In the Baraka-Dorn correspondence, you'll see the same range of reference. This takes you out of codified literary history and into actual people. Part of the point of the scholarship is to follow the person. Forget about the school. Who did the person think about? Who did they criticize? If they're criticizing someone, that person is in their sphere. They're thinking about them. They're concerned with them.

LB: They might be more concerned with someone outside their so-called school than someone in it, but it's become unfashionable, when performing literary history, to focus on individuals rather than movements and trends. Those kinds of handles are useful ...

AA: Of course, but they're also limiting.

LB: Yes. A few times now, you've mentioned individual students who have edited an installment of *Lost and Found*. Can you talk, broadly, about the students' role in the project and how it serves as a training ground for them?

AA: I've noticed several things about the general trajectory of writers and poets working in academia in the US over the last thirty to forty years, but especially over the last twenty. I don't want to be too harsh, but they often exhibit a certain kind of ambivalence or contempt for the academic structure they exist in. A poet writing a "tenure book" is really disturbing to me. I came into this business as a Middle East scholar and so I really appreciate the nature of scholarship. Having said that, I think a lot of the students who have shown up here have felt a dissatisfaction with some of the scholarly models that they see out there and are very attracted to the odd and unique mix we have here at the Graduate Center, which on the one hand is very writer-friendly but on the other hand is rigorous in terms of what you're going to need to think about if you're going to produce scholarship. The further back in time you go, the more prerequisites there are: if you're a Medievalist, you need some Latin, another language, this and that. If you're working in a contemporary period, you actually know the least, but you have a hard time validating what you know intuitively, which is the time that you're in. The trick is to learn the traditional skills of knowledge gathering, codification, and transmission, and then to think about the times you're in, because it's easy to think that you automatically understand something because it's contemporary.

LB: Can you discuss scholarship's relationship to the contemporary? One suggestive thing you've said elsewhere about literary scholarship is that you think the most radical work one can be doing right now is nuts and bolts contextual history. What is it about scholarship in our historical moment that makes you say something like that?

AA: That's an incredibly complicated question because there are so many levels involved. There are a couple of things I would say. I've been proofreading a project that I helped edit called *Circles and Boundaries*, by my friend Kate Tarlow Morgan, who had a lot to do with *Lost and Found*. She has written about how the category of adolescence was invented by Rousseau in the 1760s and 1770s, around the time of the steam engine. Before then, it wasn't a category: you were a child and then you worked. What has happened in this country is that we've extended this category. A high school diploma is worth nothing at this point. A college education only takes you so far. You need some kind of graduate degree. So on the one hand you have this extension of adolescence as advanced degrees become increasingly necessary. But on the other hand, the trend is for the educational process to be curtailed. People want to move through school as quickly as possible. There isn't much time for real scholarship in this career trajectory. Olson went to the Library of Congress and read every item on whaling so as to boil it down into two paragraphs for *Call Me Ishmael*. That's no longer a common occurrence. People don't have the time.

LB: I agree, but why do people feel that way? They could go slower. What creates this condition?

AA: The general terror of life as it's lived. In other words, the worry that you're going to get stuck, that you're not going to have job security, not going to be able to raise a family. There's no safety net. Even in the period of time since I finished my doctorate in 1989 — at the same university where I now teach — even in this twenty-year period, the student experience is another universe compared to the way I did it. When I first moved to New York — and this was the case up until the 1980s when it got a little dicey — it was an economy where I could work one week a month and pay the rent. Those equations have totally transformed. You're now working to live rather than living to work. In that context, it becomes exceedingly difficult to do the kind of exploratory work in which the results are unexpected and unknown. That context isn't going to change, but what I've tried to do is perforate a little bit of air into it to see what that experience would be like on a small scale and to make that the seed for a longer life's work. As opposed to the more utilitarian approach that many people have. And not surprisingly: you have loans; there are students who are first-generation college students; students coming back from the military. So people say, "Yeah, I want to finish and move on." The horizons have been curtailed enormously.

LB: I think that's a great point, but I'm wondering to what extent that sort of class-based critique is unique to students at CUNY, one of the largest city universities in the world. Are the conditions different elsewhere? Are doctoral students at, say, Harvard better funded and thus more leisured?

AA: It doesn't happen elsewhere, outside of certain very specialized disciplines. My own involvement in academia gives me a unique lens on this. My home department is Classical, Middle Eastern, and Asian Languages. To do classical Homeric scholarship, for example, you need to have studied at least French, German, and Latin to begin with. In my department, the Homeric scholar happens to be Korean and very interested in things Asian, so she also knows Chinese and Japanese. Now when you're in a tenure review and somebody from an English department, who has written a monograph on Dickens and whose research has never included any foreign sources, asks how come this Homeric scholar hasn't finished her book, you're kind of apoplectic. Well, because the learning curve is in another universe. I see it happen in other disciplines, too. Because there's a rush to produce Middle East scholars, people do not take the necessary time. You need a minimum of five years in a country to really absorb the language and other intangibles, like how a culture operates. When people are rushed through, the work is often cursory.

LB: They're getting squeezed on both ends: more education is expected of young people but in less and less time. Taking the time to do the kind of exploratory travel you did ...

AA: Yeah, I managed to cobble together about eight years in another place, Jerusalem. It qualitatively changed the nature of what I was able to do.

LB: ... seems beyond the pale of the kind of career trajectories that young people imagine are available to them.

AA: We've become so self-governing that nobody has to tell us to act a certain way because you're going to do it yourself. It's totally internalized. I see it in politics, too. After September eleventh, I was offered a weekly column called "Politics and Imagination" in a Bosnian newspaper. I was able to write there in ways that were unimaginable here. I wrote a column about when Bush went to Ground Zero, the clip of which reminded me of Milošević when he came to Gazimestan. It was the same situation: he had a bunch of handlers, he was very nervous, he didn't like the crowd, he was very apprehensive, but they threw him into the scene and he came up with a slogan and the crowd responded. And it was the same thing with Bush. So I was able to describe that, which would have been unimaginable in someplace like *The Nation* in the first weeks after September eleventh.

LB: In our discussion of *Lost and Found*, you've talked a fair bit about your background as a Middle East scholar, as a translator, and as an activist. What do you see as the relationship between that work, much of which came earlier in your career, and your more recent work on American poetry?

AA: In 2005, I was attacked by the watchdog group Campus Watch in an article called "Poetry, Terror, and Political Narcissism." There were several ironies involved in the attack, but one of the things that I found most interesting was that, after years of doing work on the Middle East, I was attacked at a time when I was more and more involved in US-based material and institutions. I don't think that's coincidental. The fact that I was bringing in issues and people from the Middle East and other parts of the world to places like the St. Mark's Poetry Project and other US cultural institutions was what cranked up the volume on the attack. The attack had some libelous stuff in it, but it was one of the greatest possible validations of my work because it meant that these reactionaries implicitly and explicitly recognized the power of culture. This made me realize that my own poetic and scholarly efforts, in terms of what I'd like to do over the next x number of years, are very much related to this continent, these poets. I feel that it's a continuation of my previous work and that it's potentially unsettling.

LB: We've talked a lot about your own career trajectory, which I think exemplifies that model of personal, poetic, and scholarly curiosity evident in the *Lost and Found* initiative, but what about younger scholars who are starting out? Given the predicaments for undertaking scholarship that you've outlined, what sorts of courses of action are possible for someone who might have these intuitions or inclinations but might not work in an environment where there are outlets or spaces for them?

AA: One very simple practical piece of advice I often give to graduate students is that, given the constraints you're under, maybe you need to think about your dissertation as simply being one chapter of a much larger trajectory which will take you many years to get to. That doesn't mean that you need to lessen your ambitions or your conceptual framework, it just means that you need to say, in practical terms, this is the amount of work that I can do at this level at this time. The idea is to develop not the amount of work but its method.

LB: How worried do you think students are about how their work fits within market concerns?

AA: I think there's a tremendous amount of self-policing that takes place for students. I've been very involved in various aspects of departmental life: chair of a department, director of a program, deputy chair of a large PhD program, involved in the job process, sat on tenure committees, search committees, and so on. People self-police. In many cases, they underestimate the collective intelligence of their colleagues who are hiring them. And sometimes they may be right to do so. But in most cases — and I've seen this proven time and again by how some of our graduates have gotten jobs — if the quality of the work, and the intent and the ethos and responsibility of the person are evident, those things will have a lot of weight in terms of how the particularities of the work will be considered. This isn't always the case, but it happens much more than you'd think.

LB: In other words, when they present their work to strangers, students don't think they're going to be granted their *donnée*.

AA: Exactly. You're fitting it to your projected idea of what you think they want, which may have no basis in reality. As opposed to saying, "This is my strength. It may sound weird to you, but let me explain." I think in many more cases than you'd think, you'll get the benefit of the doubt simply based on the strength of your own argument and the strength of the work. That's why things are so stultified: everyone's trying to conform to some idea of what they think is wanted. And the main point is that "they" are "you," just with jobs.

LB: Talking now, it occurs to me that in this very project I've set up that self-policing position as a straw man that I then knock down. But it may be necessary because I've internalized a belief in the existence of certain overly rigid external expectations. They don't exist, but I have to act as though they do so that I can grant myself permission to escape them.

AA: I don't think that's atypical at all.

LB: It might be useful at this point to articulate briefly the connection between this interview and my own project. I'm very interested in the similarities between the interview as a form and a scholarly project like *Lost and Found*, in that both perform intellectual labor in large part by moving information from one place to another.

AA: I discovered that in my book *Keys to the Garden*. To me the centerpiece of that book is the interviews, which are there in place of an essay: they're historical, they're biographical, they're political, they're aesthetic.

LB: They *are* an essay.

AA: They're an essay.

LB: My other goal in conducting this interview was to help make information about *Lost and Found* available to readers who might not have otherwise encountered it. Can you talk about what its reception and dissemination has been like to this point?

AA: It's pretty surprising what's happened. It was published in an edition of 1,000 and 500 which sold out in the space of several months. They're now available through the Center for the Humanities, Small Press Distribution, and in certain bookstores. The hardest part about distribution has been creating the list of places where they would be sold because to me that is the whole business. The first hit was among people to whom this stuff really matters, to whom this history is personal and important. Through word of mouth and other means, most of those people have gotten it, which gives this project a firm basis of existence. I was driving, for example, from San Francisco to LA and got a phone call from Graham Mackintosh, a close friend of Jack Spicer, founder of White Rabbit Press, and a printer for Black Sparrow Press. Graham said he hadn't seen anything like this in years — I almost drove off the highway. When I conceived of this project, if I had a pair of eyes that I wanted to look at it, they were his. As object, it passed muster: the rest will take care of itself.

LB: Are they available digitally, too?

AA: We've gone Luddite and old school on this for the time being. The general consensus was that there is something important about maintaining it as a print publication.

LB: I guess the other function an interview might serve — though I don't think this always happens — the other function it can serve in addition to bringing the work to a larger audience is that it can deepen the work's background for those already familiar with it.

AA: My feeling about it is that there is no audience. There's you, there's me, there's who we give it to — there's no abstract audience. The audience is very particular. It's people who actually receive it. I can go into numerous examples. When I came back from Jerusalem, right before the Gulf War, after living there for about six years, I was being encouraged to write about the experience for the *Sunday Times Magazine*, but chose not to because I didn't think it was a good idea. Around that same time, Robert Creeley got in touch and said he'd been invited to Jerusalem, what did I think he should do? I told him to go, but to let me write him something about what he should be looking for because nobody's going to show it to you. I wrote him this long letter, called "Israel-Palestine 101," which I later published with his permission in *Memories of Our Future*. Writing that letter had so much more efficacy than if I had written something for the *Times*, which a week later would have been fish wrapping. The letter went to an individual who absorbed it, internalized it, did something with it.

LB: I've been fascinated lately by the letter as a literary form and its one-to-one model of intellectual exchange as a stage for preliminary thinking, or for thinking that calls itself preliminary but is actually the thing itself.

AA: There's a great line in Ralph Maud's *Olson at the Harbor* where he talks about seeing Olson wiped out one day and asking him what he had been doing and Olson said, "I wrote eight letters today." Everything gets worked out in those letters.

LB: Olson's *Maximus Poems* begins as letters to Vincent Ferrini. And a lot of the material you're republishing in *Lost and Found* is letters.

AA: We write hundreds of emails per week. What happens to them?

LB: I used to write emails as though they were letters, especially when email first came into existence. But I feel like that's discouraged. It takes time to exchange letters.

AA: I have a couple of handwritten correspondences and you really have to gear up for them. It's a very exciting thing. It's a very different thing than on the screen.

LB: There's a material object involved. I just started a handwritten correspondence with a friend and even knowing the first letter was going to arrive, it still felt surprising to receive something in the mail that wasn't related to commerce.

AA: In his *History of Textual Scholarship*, David Greetham has a great thing where he says that what we think of as normal manuscript material is a very rare, short-lived phenomenon. The existence of a manuscript is generally not the case: the originals used to be destroyed after a printing. The period of the typewriter manuscript is rare and anomalous. So in a weird way the model that we're on now may be closer to a historical precedent. It's an unsettling and weird and useful thing to know. It complicates all sorts of things. It's odd that we have a manuscript of *The Waste Land* with Pound's scribblings on it. We don't have that for the Elizabethan period.

LB: What you're talking about is a great example of the kind of insight that only historically-minded, contextually-rich scholarship can provide. How do you see your work — both in *Lost and Found* and elsewhere — in relation to regnant models of historical literary scholarship, be it New Historicism or whatever is in its wake?

AA: That's a big question. Let me try to answer it with an example. I just discovered that Christopher Simpson's *The Science of Coercion* is out of print. It's a great, concise history of Cold War propaganda, with no punches pulled. When I assign this book to graduate students — who are of course familiar with Foucault — I ask them how they can glean its methodology, which is not evident.

LB: It's not "using" Foucault.

AA: It's not "using" anything. How do you discern its methodology? Simpson's book demonstrates everything one could find in Foucault as far as his research methods, the interrogation of institutional structures, the archaeology of knowledge, but it doesn't wear its Foucauldianism on its sleeve.

LB: Why do you think that is and what might its implications be?

AA: There's been a complicated shift in what for want of a better term might be called "bourgeois liberal thought," which has adopted theory, but decontextualized it. All of this theory grew out of decolonization. When people were talking about the Other in the '50s, they were talking about the Algerian. When they were talking about the body, they were talking about the tortured body.

LB: So you're saying that as this theory has been imported, its original context has fallen away.

AA: It gets imported at the cost of poetics, at the cost of the thought of poetics. There's no poetry in any of this stuff. Ed Dorn had some very provocative and useful diatribes against continental theory in *Ed Dorn Live*, his last interviews. The problem is that if you're French, you've grown up in an education system where certain philosophical postulates are a given, so that when you encounter Derrida, it's completely logical, it comes at the end of a long train of thought. But that's not true in an American context.

LB: That was my own experience as an undergraduate being introduced to literary theory. I was given recent theory without knowing much, if anything, about the history of work whose shoulders it stood on.

AA: It's hard to read Derrida if you haven't read Benveniste, for example. You don't know the philological background to the thought, so you're getting an abstraction of it. It's very depressing. People have been brainwashed into accepting all this terminology and its application. It's incredibly brilliant, but its usefulness depends on what you're doing with it. When you encounter something like *The Science of Coercion*, which doesn't fit into the received categories of theory, you don't know what to do with it. You have to encounter that text on your own. You have to reach a state of consciousness where the text will impinge upon your assumptions. I often teach Amiri Baraka's *Blues People* in the context of literary theory and it takes a while for students to figure out why since it seems more like a work of sociological history. But Baraka says in the preface that it is a theoretical work.

LB: That kind of approach to a text seems to me a poetic one. How does your own background as a poet inform your scholarship? Someone unfamiliar with your work might hear that you're a poet and think that means, say, that you write well-crafted sentences in your criticism. Which may be true. But what you've been saying about poetry as a mode of thought that has been, in a North American context, an alternative to canonical literary theory seems much more substantial than a concern with matters of superficial aesthetics.

AA: The reality of the US is incredibly complicated. In *The Book of the Fourth World*, Gordon Brotherston revisits the famous Levi-Strauss-Derrida debate about the speech-writing hierarchy and concludes that they're both wrong because neither of them deal with non-written texts, which is what he's dealing with in the pre-Colombian Americas: quipus and other texts that don't fit that model. For all the work I've done on the Middle East, there's no comparison to the levels of complexity that you find here, in the context of the indigenous cultures and peoples of the Americas before and then through the colonial encounter.

LB: That's a really surprising statement because the politics of the Middle East are typically perceived as hopelessly complicated.

AA: Stereotypically, yes, but in fact it's all pretty readable, it's all pretty legible, because the layers are all there. But here, how do you begin to account for disappeared languages, mixed peoples? It's off the charts. Who are we? It's so complex. So to go back to your initial question, poetry is a form of knowledge that can allow you to get at that complexity. It's an approach. For my generation and the one previous, you cut your teeth on Pound's The *ABC of Reading*. When I've taught it in the past ten years, students don't know how to respond to it—Pound is a crank. But however cranky he is, there's stuff there. He's telling you to read this but don't read this, to immerse yourself in this and that and understand how meter works. He's telling you actual stuff. It's not theory.

LB: *ABC* is off-putting, too, because there's very little commentary in the anthology at the end. It's just given to you.

AA: Yeah, *you* figure it out. I think theory is a kind of prophylactic. It removes the need to make judgments. People are very afraid of two things: generalizing and making judgments. Because they're risks. But if you're not making judgments, you're hiding the authoritarianism behind these theoretical constructs and you're dismissing authority, which is needed. You can go to Pound as both an authoritarian and as an authority.

LB: Yeah, the problem isn't the exercise of authority, because we want to be able to say certain things in the past are good and worth preserving and thinking about in a continuum with the present, but what's troubling is what you were just saying about hiding the power relations, not making them open and apparent. It's like a cocktail: two parts Butler, one part Foucault, one part Stein, and you have your argument.

AA: Take something like Muriel Rukeyser's *Willard Gibbs*. First of all, she had to teach herself high mathematics in order to be able to write about Gibbs. Second, she was criticized for daring to say that the representative people of the nineteenth century were Melville, Whitman, and Gibbs. But if you make a claim like that, you're going to elicit a response, you're taking a risk. When I talk about Charles Olson as a major thinker of the twentieth century, people are going to look at me like I'm a lunatic. It's like when I gave a talk at Cornell on poetry and politics, the first thing I did was to ask how many people are familiar with Robert Duncan. Maybe two hands. Then I asked how many people are familiar with Michel Foucault? The whole room. Why is that? What's at work here?

LB: Two things that strike me. One is that running throughout many of your remarks is a do-it-yourself ethos. The other, which seems crucial, is that what you're doing by asking those questions at the start of your Cornell talk—and this is something many writers and scholars I admire do—is that you're creating a context for your work that doesn't already exist but that needs to, for one reason or another. That's the thing, actually, about the codification of literary theory: it allows you to assume you're operating within the exact same intellectual context as your colleagues. Which is of course never the case. I don't want to make it into too much of an equation, but an important aspect of *Lost and Found* is the way in which it creates a context you consider vital, but which can't be assumed as shared by others.

AA: Absolutely. In this case, I don't know where it's going to lead. Marilyn Hacker sent a nice email where she said she was happy to see Rukeyser in this context because she belongs there. Rukeyser's never thought of in relation to New American Poetry, but she's related. And so when I say *Lost and Found* considers New American Poetry "writ large"—in and around and about—that's to avoid reducing these writers to a series of schools: Black Mountain, New York, the Beats. These were movements, yes, but they were like an enormous scattering of magnetic filings. Kerouac is a great example of the need for context. There's a scene in *On The Road* where he's driving through an obviously black neighborhood and the scene is a kind of projection. Discussing this scene in class, a student said that it was racist. Well, look at the next page, where he's doing the same thing to a farm. Maybe he was racist, but what does that mean? In what context? Who was he with? What music did he know, inside and out? If you've ever listened to Kerouac read his "History of Bop," you'll be astounded at some of the phrases: "America's inevitable Africa," for instance. Amiri Baraka has Kerouac's books around his house, all over the place, including all the new stuff that's come out. That kind of critique makes me crazy. It's so easy; it's so simple, so lazy.

LB: It's not judgment.

AA: It's not judgment. It's received opinion and it's conformism. It's like the patriarchal and misogynistic business with Olson. Yeah, the guy was very problematic. On the other hand, think about it in reverse, what does it mean for a guy who was 6'7", with a successful political career, to say, "I'm outta here. I'm a poet." The only thing it could mean is that he's a fag. It's the only thing it could mean in that context. You don't think he overcompensated for that?

LB: Creeley talks, in "Contexts of Poetry," the first *Lost and Found* pamphlet, about the physical fact of Olson, how he didn't want the attention, but it was unavoidable with his height.

AA: Instead of this retrograde thing why not apply Lacan's gaze? Or "being for others"? He was noticed. You could do a Fanonian or Lacanian reading of Olson, but instead you get this simplistic thing.

LB: It merely replicates what you already know about certain power structures.

AA: It's not helpful. It doesn't advance anything. It puts him in his place, so you don't have to deal with him, instead of complicating things and asking what it might mean that his work was so liberating for all these female poets.

LB: The irony of many applications of theory is that they take this incredibly rich, nuanced, and textured discourse and completely flatten out its implications.

AA: Derrida has wonderful readings of Edmund Jabès, really nuanced and intricate. You can't reapply them elsewhere, though. They're great in and of themselves, but that's it. The only thing you could do would be to reapply their intent.

The Clinamen

Notebook Excerpts

: Context

The following chapter excerpts some of my preliminary notes for this project.

: What was I trying to do?

I could cite numerous rationales for including these notes for the book as part of the book itself — they show how the sausage got made, they add another layer of recursion to an already recursive book, they evidence my lax attitude toward the use of constraint — but, more than anything, I'm coming, as a dedicated note taker, to understand notebooks as the place where the personal abuts the intellectual. Reading notebooks constitute a form of intellectual autobiography that, even when absent of personal detail, has as its foundation the note taker's personal autobiography, the life being lived as the notebook gets toted here and there. As with any base-superstructure relationship, even the subtlest of alterations to the unseen foundation can have dramatic consequences for what gets built on top of it.

Notebook Excerpts

5/5/07
high-wire feats of literary constraint (*Never Again, Eunoia*) perhaps obscure more mundane applications of it

(me)
thinking consists
of funny spaces, stops
interruptions, revelations
▼
hence poetry

6/6/07
Sanders' catalogue of ships problem: how to avoid "data-midden boredom"

6/7/07
(me) can restrictions be seen as a way of dealing w/ Olson's problem of the postmodern (quantitative overload)?

6/8/07
(me) the critic takes everything on what she imagines to be the terms by which they must be engaged — ie, history, the invisible arbiter, tradition, etc.
– the artist takes everything on her own terms and in so doing defines the rules of engagement better than the critic ever can

6/10/07
(me) to be listless is to sink into a state of lethargy from lack of the governing sense of order and purpose that a list provides

distinction:
1) appositive list—amplify & refine
2) enumerative, or itemized, list—collect, set down
    another distinction, within enumerative lists:
    a) indefinite series: can continue indefinitely, unbounded as long as you're able to think of new entries
    b) definite series: has a prescribed # of entries, a boundary

6/17/07
DHL. *Mornings in Mexico*
p. 77—"Our cosmos is a great engine. And we die of ennui."

6/20/07
(me) think about Sanders' catalogue of ship's problem in relation to what Stein says about naming as a poetic act in "Poetry and Grammar"

6/22/07
the asymptote & the list

6/23/07
Zukofsky & the Oulipo, esp. Roubaud
– Perloff essay on the topic

6/24/07
(me) the asymptote as the way knowledge works

(me) consider the list as a genre
– does it have a history?
– key practitioners?
– developments? breakthroughs? etc.

(me) list & the Oulipo
– renunciation of chance procedures indicates a desire for total mastery, the illusion that rigid constraint, and lists, provide

(me) what to say about lists other than that they are essential
– the history of lists is a history of doing, of planning & failing to do

6/26
(me) cannot overstate the importance of the fact that the Oulipo claims one of their principal aims is the creation of constraints for any writer to use
– the thrust of most literary / artistic movements: exclusion—this is what makes us new, different, revolutionary, inimitable, or imitable only insofar as the imitation is perforce unoriginal, inferior
– *in the Oulipo, imitation — of themselves, of others — is a virtue*
– there are no contests for primacy, for supreme originality, for genius

— reading Bénabou's *Why I Have Not Written Any of My Books* & becoming aware of the way in which Oulipians are writers who know they want to be writers before they know what it is they want to write (like myself)
▸ thus, the form over content tendency (Mathews' essays esp.). Thus, the tendency of so many books to dwell — explicitly, allegorically, symbolically, etc. — on the act of writing
    – writing for writing's sake

6/27/07
Bénabou equates reading as he does it to bulimia

6/29/07
(me) the use of "etc." when, in fact, you've run out of things to say
    – the reluctant exhaustion of a list

7/6/07
for the prospectus: by not extending constraint to the critical realm, the Oulipo implicitly reinforces the notion that there is an unbridgeable gulf b/t the creative & the critical
    – I imagine this project as a living critique of that notion

7/12/07
Stein's a vocabulary can't not make sense quote

7/15/07
(me) all classificatory systems, if followed through far enough, ultimately reveal their own inadequacies
    – Mathews' *The Journalist* a parable of the endpoint of all classification

8/6/07
Kubler: "By this view, the great differences b/t artists are not so much those of talent as of entrance & position in sequence."
    ▼
        might be relevant to anticipatory plagiary
    ▼
in this view, a way of dealing w/ the problem of arriving too late in the series/sequence

8/7/07
Jefferson's *Notes* as a possible precursor, an ordering exercise
– Deist god is a clock-maker
– Oulipians become clock-makers

8/9/07
genealogies at the end of the *Popol Vuh*?

8/14/07
Rukeyser's Gibbs bio?
– scientific methods
– p. 350: quote on math

Stein, in "Poetry and Grammar"
p. 238: language is an "intellectual recreation"
▶ (me) both leisure/play & re-create

WCW's thoughts on Poe: local b/c he establishes his own rules, makes clearing & foundational gestures—might be relevant to Oulipo

The Cat in the Hat & *Green Eggs & Ham* both written w/ the restriction of a vocab list, à la Mathews' *Selected Declarations* (a proverb list)

8/15/07
Poe's "Philosophy of Criticism" makes me realize that you can distinguish b/t intentional (Cage) & unintentional (inspiration, intuition, automatic writing) chance, the former being a type of constraint, the latter not

8/16/07
(me) Nufer & Bök both write wild sex passages

8/22/07
(me) why does Mathews say in *The Paris Review* that he got the idea for *Singular Pleasures* from an angel while he was jetlagged? Mocking or serious?
(me) a distinction suggests itself: inspiration can make you want to do something but is not enough to make you actually do it
> that is, the Oulipo isn't against inspiration per se, but against the idea of inspiration as the modus operandi of artistic creation
– Oulipo: creation is pure labor, nothing divine about it
i.e., Bök was inspired by the Oulipo to come up with his book idea, but what enabled him to persevere & write the book was the constraint, not the inspiration
– in other words, there is a place for inspiration in the Oulipian worldview, it is just a much more limited one than we ordinarily imagine it to be
QED

8/27
(me) what makes a list authoritative?

---

meeting w/ Wayne — 9/4

– argument, overarching
– self-diagnosis of my method
– horror & restraint
– lots of work done on lists
– think of prospectus as a manifesto — polemic
– who are you trying to convince out of what torpor

Books—9/4
I Remember   *Alphabetical Africa*
queerness   Sorrentino

    Poe
    Roussel
    theory / manifesto

    MATH
    LOGIC   X20
    THOUGHT
    WRITING AS SEX

Mathews:
   Singular Pleasures   *Sleeping w/ the Dictionary*
   20 Lines   *Eunoia*
   Selected Declarations   *Fortification Resort*
   Cigarettes   *Never Again*
   The Journalist   *Negativeland*

Cage   French Oulipo   what are they bored w/?
they're bored w/ sex, broadly construed
— that is, sex is consumerism, is channeled desires, is trying to escape those desires, is the dialectic of availability, of choice that the quantitative inundates us w/

issues
— translation
— sex
— play/games
— the exercise
— chance
— bondage/constraint
— order, classification
— lists
— horror, trauma
— masturbation, pleasure, self-pleasure

sex

parts of speech & sex
latent in founding Oulipians
explicit in 2nd generation Americans
"clinamen" sounds vaguely sexual
desire in the modern world: unlike knowledge, it's not an asymptote: is too readily catered to and fulfilled
rigid sex—analytical dictionary definitions—math
awkward sex—Brainard
periphrasis
lists—spillage
death & sex
compounds, kennings
Poe—banishment of sex
Roussel—jouissance—Barthes
    – do I have to do deal w/ this?
X20—desire—pain
2nd gen'ers—sex & boredom
masturbation—closest we can get to the consummation of fantasy?—writing?
sex & pop culture—Mullen
acrobatic descriptions of sex—Nufer, Bök
games & sex
words & sex
exercise & sex
chance?
bondage, order
language

9/10/07
the constraint most people are familiar w/ is the deadline

9/12/07
for Olson, the critical act is in the choosing, prior to the analysis (from his letters to Creeley & Benedict)

9/18/07
all Oulipian texts are fundamentally about writing
> ▶ (me) an interesting corollary:
>> they don't distinguish b/t writing poetry & writing fiction, it is all, of a piece, just writing, only according to different rules

(me) implicitly, I might be making an argument about the imagination & structure, the latter as somehow essential to the former

10/12/07
Oulipians are de Certeauian users
> ▶ grasp of what is controllable for them as individuals, but not the larger situation
> – rats who devise their own maze

10/15/07
ways of organizing the bibliography:
> alphabetical, chronological, reverse alphabetical, thematic, personal preference, scrambled (arbitrary, random), reverse chronological, associative logic, number of letters in the title, Amazon sales rank
– see Perec's "Ways of Arranging My Library"

10/25/07
(me) if it's an "exercise" in criticism, then at least some of the constraints should be familiar critical modes (psychoanalysis, deconstruction, New Historicism, etc) or forms (bibliography, book review, etc)

10/26/07
Friedlander, *Simulcast*, p. 55: "the most suspicious writing of all masks its literary qualities"

(me) in a way, the real point of Friedlander's exercise is Welch's point vis-à-vis Stein: that grammar & sentence structure & rhythm have their own emotional and argumentative force

11/25/07
(me) constraint as a prosthesis?
– related to androcentrism?

1/22/08
(me) chance procedures not as egoless-ness (avant-garde radicalness) but as a submission to fate (gambling)

1/22/08
(me) literary criticism is the only art criticism that partakes in the same medium as its object of study
– think of how frustrating most music criticism is in the translation from sound to word

1/23/08
(me) a faux-reverential scholarly ch.
– Borgesian

1/24/08
(me) make Ex in Crit my one main book that I keep expanding and revising, like *Leaves of Grass* and other 19th C. works of accretion (Douglass' autobio), like *Maximus* & that line of lifelong poems

(me) like Perec says about the lipogram, constraints always need to announce themselves as such, lest they go unnoticed
– could be a justification for revealing the constraint / methodology

– doesn't satisfy a curiosity but declares an allegiance

Huizinga, p. 8: play "is free, is in fact freedom"

1/28/08
(me) exercise is always very structured, esp. at the professional level

4/8/08
for meeting w/ Wayne

publication
I feel
too scattershot at the moment — need to tackle some major issues now,
prospectus — ok
definition
loose constraints ok? (more severe, more exciting, if I can pull it off)
freedom, discourses of — America

Meeting w/ Wayne

prefatory — constraint & book & constraint I'm using
– graphic — t.o.c.

pretend that it's a biblio

find constraints that don't . . .

interrupt sameness — anything you can do to interrupt claustrophobia

literary & cultural history to define constraint
– tonal & procedural family resemblance
dispositif: proscenium that the . . .

overview of issues for 2nd half of prospectus

some cuts in *I Remember* ch.
   – put some back — a system

6/17/08
Hotel Theory—a ch. on constraint applied after the fact, not beforehand—what, if anything, is the effect?

Notes as I approach the mid-point and do some spring cleaning, 4/09

– Wittgenstein: "When I obey a rule, I do not choose. I obey the rule blindly."
   p. 72, *Philosophical Investigations*

– a ch. of deliberately misguided interpretations
– a ch. where the constraint is complete freedom
– ch. w/ no commas, but no Steinian run-ons

– Oulipo & amateurs

– Huizinga, p. 8: "Play is free, is in fact freedom."

– Carla Harryman: essay: an attempt to think about something incompletely
– Bök & exhaustion: obscure words, tiresomeness, physical exertion of his sound poetry
– deliberately misinterpret a passage from '*Pataphysics*—p. 39, for ex.
– philosophy—its rules, laws, border controls, etc—as a constraint, as constrained thinking
– philosophers (Kant, ie) as the biggest perverts, the kinkiest, most submissive writers

▼
critics: dilettante philosophers
me: dilettante critic

– a constraint about ineffective/ugly constraints, about constraints that don't lead anywhere useful?
– a constraint: you can revise, but only your first time through the essay ▶ after a paragraph (maybe a sentence?) has been completed, it cannot be altered
– Lynn Crawford's *Fortification Resort* as a non-evaluative—an ecstatic—criticism

– one possible way of doing it: where the object moves you, as opposed to what it "says"
– another: what the object "says," rendered ecstatically, done w/ oblique exposition

▼

maintains its ties to criticism more than the former in that it still serves a critical function and not simply an aesthetic one

job letter
first draft of prospectus
list of omitted books
fear of success
pan MD's book?
K. Silem
Waldrop. *A Key*
Powell
Nowak
list of potential future projects
dramatic sestinas / Writhing Society
Berrigan—sonnets
a filler ch.
Twitter
a ch. on my financials, after Myles?
p. 261 and 263 in *Wanderlust*: complicating the notion of exercise
interview myself
maybe's
Kunkel essay and Internet commentary
the "like" button on Facebook
AK's "how to" of networking for poets—blech
an epigraph for every ch.
orals list
McCaffery
find Hazlitt quote about not being able to read novels after the age of 30
what about Mac Low resists being discursively situated?
Harper's p. 17: Facebook's database reality
6-word bios—NPR
ch. written while high?
the "no one can be expelled from the Oulipo" rule as related to the

Writhing Society's mission
something on the difficulties of writing about the contemporary:
– you have to read a lot of second-rate work
– difficulty of making accurate pronouncements
– *hardest* thing—yet also the most exciting—is that the field keeps expanding right in front of you
describe an art gallery but not the art—ie, the labyrinthine Struth exhibit at the Met
a ch. where I analyze books I haven't read but claim to have
Poe's duration of a sitting
blogs

An Oulipolooza: *from* the Q&A

: Context

"An Oulipolooza" was a celebration of potential literature held at the University of Pennsylvania's Kelly Writer's House. In addition to constraint-based finger food, the event featured a panel of five scholars and poets — Katie Price, Jean-Michel Rabaté, Gerald Prince, Nick Montfort, and myself — giving readings and talks on Oulipo and literary constraint. This chapter excerpts a snippet of the panel's Question and Answer segment.

: What was I trying to do?

vAn Oulipolooza: *from* the Q&A

LOUIS BURY: I'm inclined to say a word in favor of failure   thinking of it   as a writer   as   first   an inevitability   and second   as a good inevitability   as a sign that you're doing something right   that if you're taking risks and failing   I'm also a professional poker player   so I'm used to thinking in terms of risk and if you're taking risks   as a writer or as a whatever   that means some of them aren't going to work out   and that's okay   but if you make enough bets   if you're a gambler and you make enough winning bets   that is   bets where the odds are in your favor   then in the long run you're going to come out ahead   in other words the fact that you're sometimes failing is what enables the possibility for your continued success

JEAN-MICHEL RABATÉ: do you think your work on Oulipo helps make you a successful gambler

LB: heh heh   it helps for both if you have slight OCD   but more seriously   in one way they're very different skill sets   writing is so much more intellectually complex and challenging   but in another way they're very similar in that constraints winnow down your choices and thus turn writing   almost   at least   into a kind of logic problem   playing poker at a professional level is 75% logic problem and 25% psychology problem   with psychology becoming

important where logic reaches its limits   so for example if you're writing without using the letter e and you need to use the word "poem" you have to run through a rolodex of potential synonyms until you find a solution   and maybe the substitute word you arrive at then forces you to change other parts of the sentence or paragraph in a similar way   in other words   whereas if you were just writing as normal your word choice would be purely a matter of taste and sensibility when writing with constraints your word choice becomes a matter of taste and sensibility *within the confines of available choices*   and that search for a solution within a narrowed set of choices is   for me at least   a process of logical deduction that resembles the poker thought process

One should not try to go over the limit

: Context

Midway through this project, in the course of a group conversation at a cocktail party, I happened to mention, in passing, that my father is an electrical engineer. Sensing that this seemingly innocent biographical detail might relate to my interest in constraint, Wayne Koestenbaum suggested I write about my father, electrical engineering, and constraint as part of the project. The suggestion appealed to me but the prospect of writing directly on the topic didn't, so I asked my father if he would be willing, as his birthday present to me that year, to answer a written questionnaire. I had intended to use the questionnaire, both my questions and his responses, as raw material for some future, as-yet-undetermined procedure, but the completed questionnaire felt more than self-sufficient, felt, in fact, as though tampering with it, aside from some minor reformatting, would disturb the halting equilibrium into which we had settled over the years.

: What was I trying to do?

What I was trying to do, in essence, throughout this entire project: to go over the limit by means of my own limitations.

One should not try to go over the limit

Write down a word that comes to mind when you think of yourself.
precise

What language do you think in?
It is hard to tell. I think that I am still translating from Polish to English. Sometimes when I work with numbers, I might count in Polish. I acquired very good background in Polish language with good writing skills. In high school on the last final exam in Polish a student is not allowed to make an orthographical error. If this could happen, a student must repeat the entire year.

Maybe they have different rules today not like in 1964.

Do you think differently in different languages?
Yes, of course. I still make many mistakes when I translate from Polish to English. For example the verb might be located at different part of the sentence.

Meditate on the ways in which math is like a language.
If you analyze logic circuits, one can say that this is like a language.

Does your heart thrill at the thought of an AND gate?
I don't find myself excited by working with gates. For me this is just a tool to analyze combinational or sequential logic circuits. My students find digital circuits easier to comprehend than analog. Generally, I don't like digital circuits. I prefer analog where my doctoral thesis is primary based on it.

How would you characterize your childhood?
I pleasantly remember my childhood. I had lots of freedom since my parents were both working.

I played outside from morning to evening. Many hours I played soccer (I have to account for many broken windows) or in the wintertime I was ice-skating on the lakes. I also played many war games, since this was the postwar era. I spent more time with my father than my mother. I went with him hunting, traveling, and camping, gardening etc. Every summer I went for a month for a summer camp. I would go to different part of Poland. I remember that the first camp was close to my town. Later on I would go to the Baltic Sea or to the mountains. This event was organized for children whose parent(s) were employed by the police.

How would you characterize your mother?
Smart and demanding. Very hard working women.

How would you characterize your father?
Smart and gentle. Very hard working man.

Explain the importance of your early childhood memories of guns.
As I mentioned above, this was a postwar era. I had access to many guns and rifles, since my father was a police officer. In our house we had many guns and rifles. As a teenager I was firing guns for fun in safe remote areas as in an old castle or army training area.

What do you think of these questions so far?
They are interesting. However, they are hardly related to the electrical engineering. As I remembered, you mentioned to me that your advisor suggested to you writing about me and my electrical engineering experience.

Write something long.
I will not write something long but I will mention to you that a colleague of mine from NJIT whom I work with at the Sarnoff Symposium writes less than I! Thirty-five year ago when I graduated as an engineer, **English/communication skills were not important as today.** At this point, I don't see a reason to take English classes in order to improve my communication skills.

Articulate your thoughts on transgression's importance.
One should not try to go over the limit as this can get him in trouble with the law.

What kind of social animal are you?
I don't like to socialize with people in bars. In my association with IEEE Princeton/Central Section I meet many people at our events. Since I am the Section Chair, Mom supports my volunteer work and

attends with me many section events because she understands the importance of this to me! She attended our awards dinner at Princeton University Prospect House or activities in Albany or Binghamton.

What appeals to you the most about electrical engineering as a scientific practice?

I was always curious how a radio or TV works. In 1961, in Poland, my parents purchased first TV and had troubles with it. I was able to repair this set by changing vacuum tubes. This was not a very difficult task, but I was interested how this TV set works.

What appeals to you the most about IEEE as social and professional association?

I am able to discuss variety of engineering topics with many engineers.

Do you wish Emily and I could speak Polish?

Yes, I do.

How come you never tried to teach Emily and me Polish?

Why do you think Mom was attracted to you?

I don't think this has any think to do with electrical engineering. Please ask Mom this question.

Do you consider yourself a riddle?

No, I don't.

Describe this project that I am working on.

It is a very difficult and challenging task, especially when you write with constraints.

Does the Second World War loom in your consciousness?

Yes, it does. When I was in Poland, only my parents were my family. My father had only one cousin in village next to town of Głogów. Both of my parents lost all of their family members in the war.

How do you feel about the practice of writing (in any language)?

I am more comfortable to write in Polish.

How do you feel about having conversations in English?
   I do this automatically and don't have any feelings.

How do you feel about having conversations in Polish?
   Not much different as a conversation in English.

Do you believe human nature is inherently evil, inherently good, or something in between?
   There are three categories. All of the above. It is a human nature.

When I was a child, I once asked you how come you didn't attend church with the rest of the family and you told me that it doesn't matter what you do but what you believe in your heart. Do you believe this? Do you believe in a God?
   I do believe what I said to you. I do believe in God, it has a power that can't be comprehended or explained.

Discuss a sublime experience you have had.

Say something about how constraints operate in writing.
   There is a limited writing with constraints. If you don't know a language well, that is also a constraint.

Say something about constraints, unrelated to writing.
   Any rules or laws that we impose on ourselves.

What is the nature of our relationship?

What do you most enjoy about watching sports? About playing sports?
   I want my team to win. I also want to win.

Soccer: is it a cultural style?
   Yes, it is. In South America or in Europe people are very involved with this sport. When we visited Italy in October, Emily chatted with shoemakers, I continue the conversation with them and asked them if

they knew Giorgio Chinaglia, an Italian soccer player who played for Cosmos. He is not popular in Italy due to a stock market scandal. However, the shoemakers respected him of his achievements on the soccer field.

Write something random here.

Describe the aesthetic dimension of mathematics.
I am not mathematician. However, I took linear algebra in college with many math majors they enjoyed many proofs. I didn't enjoy their philosophical analysis. I prefer more practical engineering approach with more definite results.

Do you worry a lot?
Not a lot. Sometimes.

Do you ever see yourself in me? in Emily?
I see more in you, perhaps because you choose the same teaching profession.

Say something about your life as a teacher.
I enjoy working with bright students, since they learn much faster. I don't have to work from 9 to 5.

Do you consider yourself to have a vocation in life?

What is your philosophy of existence?
We are visitors on the earth. The time goes too fast.

What is your favorite pierogi filling?
I like them with meat filling.

Write something purple here.
Purple flowers.

Would you say that the importance to your life of your time in Israel is disproportionate to the three years you spent there?

Yes, I agree.

What is it about electrical engineering specifically, as opposed to other types of engineering (chemical, civil, etc.) that appeals to you?

I can design a converter that everybody including other engineers can use.

If I had other engineering knowledge, I might enjoy other engineering areas.

Write something in Polish about your Polish identity, then translate it into English.

Psychoanalyze yourself, briefly.

Any thoughts on poetry?

I tried to give Grandma's poetry books by Juliusz Słowacki to Polish church.

She treasured these books, but I felt that they just taking a space.

Few days ago, before I made a call to the church, I read some of the poems.

I found these poems very enjoyable because they were rich in words that I could appreciate, not like poetry in English.

What do you think it is that makes you good at math?

I use math as a tool. After while you can become proficient in math by repeating particular operations.

In what ways are you different now from when you were forty-four? twenty-four?

When I was 24 I had no responsibilities. At 44 I had to support my family.

How much has living in the US changed you? Do you consider these changes to be for the better or for the worse?

I am accustomed to a US life. These changes are better and I couldn't live elsewhere.

However, my 18 years in Poland will be always in my memories.

I met Nobel Prize winner from Princeton University. He came to DeVry for a presentation.

He talked about his village in England where he spent his childhood. My point is that everyone remembers their childhood.

Are you easily impressed by others?

Sometimes.

How do you feel about communism?

I am glad that you don't have the experience to live under communism.

Because of that, I have the tendency to be more conservative and ignore socialistic values.

When did Grandma first tell you she was Jewish? How did you react?

I think I was 10. I was in SHOCK!

Say something else about electrical engineering.

Good profession.

Identify something that you don't like about electrical engineering.

In the US, engineers are not respected as in Europe.

What do you think is the purpose of these questions?

You never ask me many questions. I think you would like to find out more about me.

Do you have any thoughts about metaphor or simile?

What is logic? What is its importance? Its beauty?

Name a great pleasure you couldn't do without.
　　Working on the computer.

Quote a text that you are particularly fond of quoting or that speaks to you in some way.

What sorts of thing bother you?
　　I don't like to hear negative comments about me.

How do you view yourself in relation to others? Does this view change depending on the context?

Provide me with a glimpse of the logic of your imagination.

What are your thoughts on family?

Is there a relationship between shyness and constraint?
　　Yes it is. A person might have difficulty to express his thoughts.

Categorize your attitude towards your physical appearance.
　　I am not very concerned with my physical appearance.

Name something that I don't know about you that I'd be surprised to find out.

Describe the effect of classical music on your brain. Feel free to be poetic here.
　　It is relaxing.

Say something else about Grandma here.
Very independent. Went thru a lot during war.

Describe your basic political philosophy.
Anticommunist.

Discuss the relationship between chess and constraint.
You have to use logic in both.

Discuss the relationship between electrical engineering and constraint.
Some concepts in electrical engineering are imaginary. The constraint is that you cannot visualize them.

Discuss the relationship between masculinity and constraint.

If you weren't an engineer, you would be_____.
Science major—Geology?

Characterize your desires.
Moderate.

Are you given to introspection?

Has writing about yourself at such length had any effect on you?
Not really.

Anything else you would like to add or say.
Thanks. Lou.

To the fact, to the point, to the bottom line

: Context

The following poem consists of excerpts from my late grandmother's notebooks — original spelling and typography preserved — selected and arranged by me. Some lines in the poem, usually indicated by quotation marks, come from a conversation she and I had about her time living in the Warsaw Ghetto during the Second World War. The bolded timeline that constitutes the poem's spine comes from a letter she wrote to a friend in Israel. None of the language in the poem is my own.

: What was I trying to do?

In my early- to mid-twenties, when I had the ambition to be a writer but little actual writing to my name, people, relatives especially, would from time-to-time encourage me, on the basis of my literary ambitions, to talk with my grandmother about her experiences as a Holocaust survivor. The encouragements bothered me most when expressed as pleas to take down her stories: whatever the nature of her undisclosed experiences, I knew they were not stories. Stories were what she told my younger sister, snuggled together in the fold-out couch bed, when spending the night at my parents' house: tender reassurances of warmth and greenery and joy. Stories expressed continuity, could be passed down, cherished, caressed. What my grandmother had to tell me — and it was to me, finally, and me alone that she entrusted it, because, she said, I was a writer — what my grandmother had to tell me has only just (I can recognize, with the birth of my own son) begun to make its way through the generations as something other than a stop in the throat.

To the fact, to the point, to the bottom line

Moses Freibaum — father
Regina Hoffnung — mother

Hoffnung means "hope" in German

living in a city
living in a section
living on a street
living at ____ number
living on a floor

Ita Freibaum
Born: 27 June, 1925

brother Henjek, seven years younger
never entered school   war broke out

There are some verbs that cannot be followed by an infinitive

The effort: to afford a degree of safety

It was once a decent meaningful family life
and a happy loving childhood.
    All suddenly destroyed without a trace
       nothing left, even a single grave to turn to.
          Nothing but memories

ea = i : sea
ee = i : free see

oa = o soap
ou = u soup

nuisance — annoyance
decipher — to make clear
hominids — almost prehuman
vivacious (vaiveigies) zyzy
atonement   to atone (lo sevetie)
atoning
conciliate unspoken

To foster the desire of reading & writing
To draw conclusion

words used as nouns & verbs

answer	cry	dress
burn	dance	end
cave	demand	farm
cast	dislike	fight

The prepositions: Relationship
                with the noun

to, around, aboard, above, after,
against, along, at before, behind,
inside of off, on, beside, besides,
below, between, among.
       can be also adverbs

Who is a subject.
What can also be a subject.

Idioms
On the spur of the moment
Bend over backwards
Make ends meet
Get to the bottom of something
Bite off more than one can chew

What are you doing tomorrow?
I'll be writing my composition
A month from now I'll be living
in this apartment for 4 years

October–November 1939 long lines for bread. No electricity. No running water. The winter was severe. Our resources from before the war were used up quickly.

The adornment of wisdom is humility.
A civilisation is a distinctive form of
culture maintained through several generations.
High society.
"I am in love with my chains."
– He gave me the credit to which I have no claim.
– Simile of renewal is the snake. (serpents)
The evil with man to live after him
Your sorrow at this juncture does not concern me
His Highness the prince of.
Tendency to look away from
He generate the feeling that
– I don't like to be the recipient of his anger
– It is like chasing the rainbow
– Betray his confidence
– To the point—to the fact.
The feeling is above description
– Intellectual nutrient.
      Nourishment

Dear Wesiu Congratulation!

I am very proud of you. I always believed in you, and that's why I knew you can do Well.
I know it was not easy, but you succeed, and that what counts. Be healthy and keep up.
You have a wonderful family you get love and support.

Mom.

P.S.

I am glad my computer finely started properly and I could write my note to you tonight.
It is 11:10 P.M. I am tired but happy. nor more nerves

January 1940 I started to wear an armband with a "David Star" under strict law and punishment.

take a course *in* literature
pay attention *to*

critical of—
angry at or with me
bored with—on

Before I *left* Poland, *I'd* applied for a visa & Passport
1) simple   I left , I had
2) before   I'd left I'd had

I had been a widow before I came to the USA.

May 1940 Mr. Johan Klein, a Polish citizen before the war, a "folk-deutsch" by than, assisted by a German military police, invaded my parents home and confiscated what ever valuable things they could find. He knew my father from before the war. My father was beaten up for not opening fast enough the cabinets.

"I remember such a stupid thing which I will tell you
family cook back then was Haddassah
Haddassah liked me, always gave me food or some treat
         a piece of chocolate   a piece of candy
I remember very well:
               I would bring plates to the kitchen
                 to help Haddassah because I liked her
Regina: 'Don't do this ... Your daughter will never be a lady.'"

- sin as a *biblical* concept
- She embraced him with unguarded emotion
- The devil is not so black as he is painted
- In term of negative result
- It was subject of interest
- To a degree that gives me a sense of sensitivity
- Time will resolve that.
- Can I have your undivided intention.
- She is not acting in a manner befitting a
- Better light a candle than curse darkness
- Death and fight for survival is the natural act of nature
- An uphill battle
- I resent the implication
- It is a terrible thing to waste the mind
- When I'll make up my decision you will be the first to know.
- I was just about telling you.
- The plans seem good
- Maybe I didn't let myself looking this way.
- Study the rules and practice the problem
- The foundation was laid
- The motivation developed
- I see myself reflected in your eyes

Better English

Imply

To imply is to hint
or express indirectly
Speaking or acting can
imply

Infer

Is to draw a conclusion
from someone's implication
Only a listener or watcher
can infer.

Ingenuously

mean open frank
candid

Ingenious

means clever
inventive

Rob

To rob is to take the
contents of something
or the possession of
someone.
To rob a desk is to
open and take what
you want.

Steal

To take the thing
(illegal) itself.
To steal a desk is to
(illegally) remove it

May

permission

Can

ability

July 1940 My teacher Regina Rawicz organized a secret class for boys and girls my age. My cousins Rachel and Miriam Frejbaum and my friends Edzia Friedman and Ada Gotlib were my classmates. After four month the class was closed. The teacher was arrested along with two boys. We studied history, math, Yidish and literature.

It was a shortage of food. Ration cards were less than the minimum. I think it was about 100 gram of bread for a person daily. To buy in the market was too expensive. We started to feel hunger. I went upstate Warsaw, first, with my mother, to bring food. The ghetto was not closed, but Jews were not allowed to leave the Jewish quarters. As I could pass for a Polish looking girl, and my Polish language hadn't a scintilla of a Jewish accent, I felt that I was the one who supposed to help.

By the end of 1940 the Jewish police was founded. They stood at the gates with the German, and Polish police, while the brick wall was build with barbed wire and sharp glass on the top. My way out of the ghetto was closed.

My grandfather, my father, and his brother lost the dairy business on the Plac Kazimierza Wielkiego which was the Aryan side now. They couldn't get out anything from there. It was completely taken away when the ghetto border was implemented.

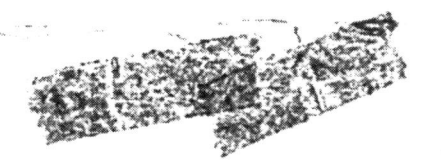

Arbeitskarte

für Arbeitskräfte

aus dem Generalgouvernement

und

Bescheinigung

über eingezahlte Lohnersparnisse

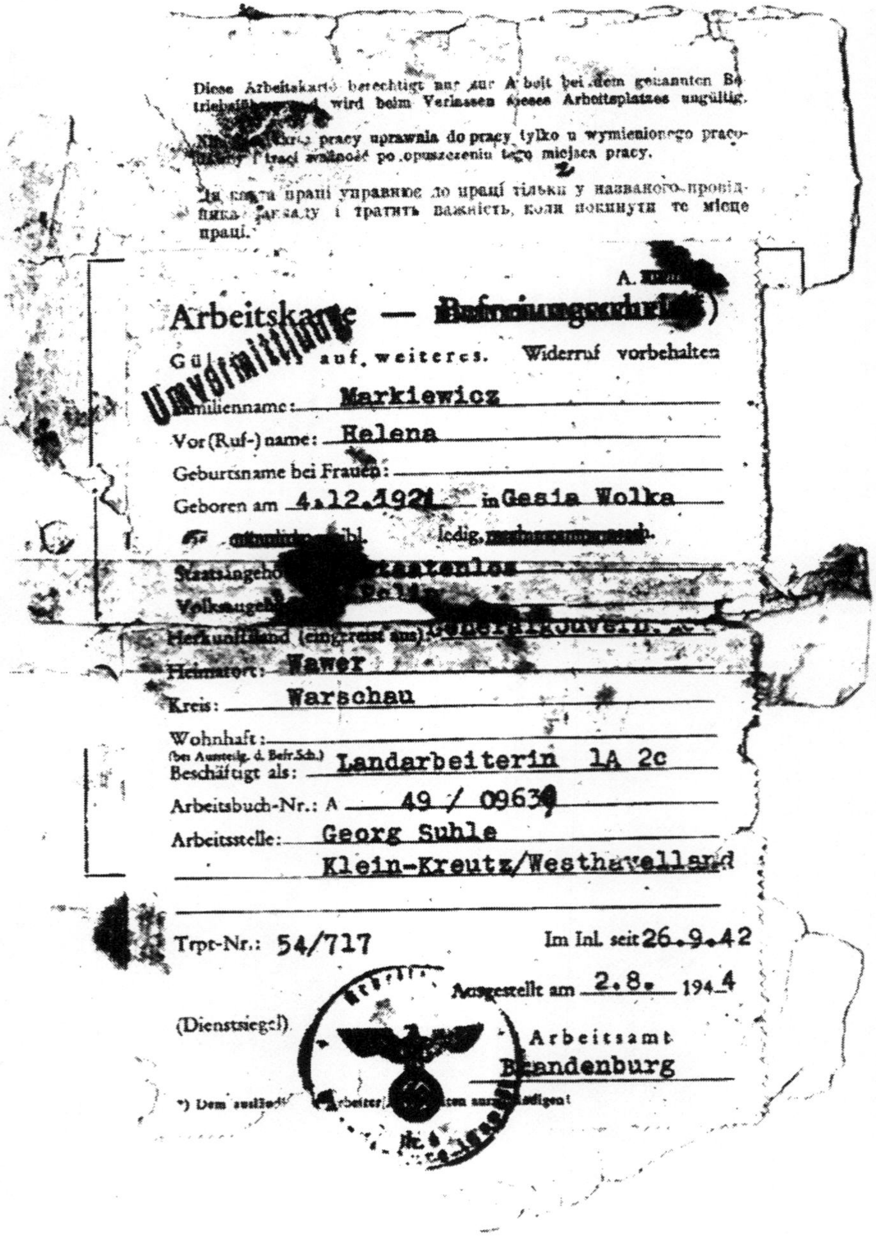

Memorandum

Date: March 16, 1998
Subject: Social Arrangement

From:
    Name: Helena Goodman
    Phone number: 253-1129
    E-mail:

To:
    Name: Mr. Melvin Katz
    CC:

Notes: I would like to make some changes in our social arrangement, that means that as long as you reside in Valley Stream we wouldn't be able to meet every week. However as soon as you move to Brooklyn the whole situation will change, and we will be able to meet as much as it will be possible. I am sure you understand the difficulties in traveling for you as well as for me. Take care and be healthy!

– He created the seeds for his own distraction.
– Agreed in principal.
– Referring to the fact.
–
– How to live up to my image
– He is reticent
– He is excessively inquisitive
– He looks ragged and poverty stricken
– On the spur of the moment
– Bend over backwards
– Make ends meet
– Bite off more than one can chew
– Meet someone half way
    I did nothing special
    I didn't do anything special
– One good term deserves another
– to get by   To take hold on
– A tit for a tat
– He is very prowessful.
– Social codes prevail

March 1941 the food ration was smaller, we were hungry. We could not afford to buy on the black market.

Intellectual stimulation
I realized with delight how happy I am. —

– Anticipate with a degree of anxiety

– He was not up to a losing battle for a principle

– renewed vitality

– I have derived security from the certain and known sources

– Never had a jewish education in sense of orthodox religious

interminable long.
admonished serenely

– natural intense
– Time and patience

Motivated by fear
– The magnitude of
– Hypothetic question

– My growing sense of lost (not to share)
Invented tactical decisions.

– To assess a situation

– To play and act who you are not.

– It is no use of thinking this way

– Perished in this preposterous

Like a new pair of shoes a pleasure to put on and pain to wear

– Human endeavor

Literature
Thomas Mann. *A Sketch of My Life.*
Simone de Beauvoir.
Raquel. *The Jewess of Toledo.*
Blind Faith. by Joe McGinniss.
Golda Meir: Woman of Valor.
Maimonides.
For The Record. Donald T. Regan
How the Jewish People Live Today. by Mordecai T. Soloff.
1962. *Camille: The study of Claude Monet.* by C. P. Weekes.
Behind the Silken Curtain. Bartley C. Crum
Arab. Jaamal Husseini
François Mitterand. 1996
Thomas Jefferson. by John Severance
Emily Dickinson. by Bradley Steffens
The Making of a Jew. Edgar Bronfman
Howard Fast. *Redemption.* 1996.
Carl Sagan. Ellen R. Buth & Joyce Schwartz
Mark Twain. Richard B. Little
The Hidden Pope. Darcy O'Brien
Dwight David Eisenhower. Marian G. Cannon
Wait Till Next Year. Doris Kearns Goodwin.
The Buck Stops Here. Morrie Greenber.
Belva Plain. *Fortune's Hand.*
Julius Caesar. Roger Bruns, A. M. Schlesinger Jr.
Chaim Potok. *The Chosen.*
Eleonore Roosevelt: The Reluctant First Lady. Loraine Hickie.
Isaac Bashevis Singer: Lost in America
My Life with Dreiser. by Helen Dreiser
Song of the Valley. Sholem Asch.
Ted Kennedy: The Legend and Tragedy. Max Lerner.
Mary Higgins Clark. *"A Cry in the Night"*
Black Velvet Gown. Catherine Cookson
Kathleen Kennedy. by Lynne McTaggart
Bright Star of Exile.
Georges Simenon
Calvin Tomkins. *Living well is the best revenge.*
Howard Fast. *The Immigrants.*
Kissinger. Marvin Kalle

July 1941 I attended a sewing course organized by ORT, by Mrs. Roma Brandes at Leszno Street, in order to report to work knowing a trade.

Dear Marianne.

Thank you enormously for the birthday present "Beyond Stich & Bitch" I like it very much. It is fun to read the stories, and confirm what I always felt; that it is much more behind the ball of yarn and a pair of needles.

It brings reflection. It takes one back to the first uncoordinated struggle with the needles to a surprisingly flow of rows of knitting. Self designed, and scientifically calculated; what a trill! Anyway, the fingers do the work, but the thoughts are free to wander the other way. Call it meditation or relaxation. It doesn't matter. Strange how a mundane work can ease stress.

It is also good to find out that there are more fanatics and addicts to yarn. It justified my own. I feel like I was sitting in a doctor's waiting room with patients of the same illness. That makes someone feel much better.

Thank you again for a thoughtful present.
Love Mom.

Conditional Phrase
If I can I will
If I could I would

I wish I could better.
I hope I'll learn soon.
She hopes to be able to do it.

If I were you I would do it.

If I did know I would not go there.

"I was on my own. I was alone."

1939 in Otwock there lived over 14,000 Jews, making up about 70 percent of all inhabitants. In 1939, at the beginning of the occupation, Germans burned down Otwock synagogue. During the fall of 1940 they created a ghetto. On August 19th, 1942 a liquidation of the Otwock ghetto had started. The Germans shot about two thousand people; almost seven thousand were transported to the death camp in Treblinka. In Karczew the Germans created a labor camp for Jews. Most of the prisoners were killed at the end of 1942.

Between elation and despair
Therapeutive talk
Inability to feel Pleasure
Fey satisfaction
Hides fear of social and
intellectual embarrassment
It is relatively small, but adequate
in depicting the essence aspect
Recapture the past
equaniminity
Money corrupted by democracy
Mutation in attitude

Evolutionary imprint
Altruism and exploitative instinct

What can I still believe in?
I want to know. I want to know

deviate — turn aside
aberration — deviate from normal acti
Ambivalent — uvepezy
Abate   become less
obviate — zopolenc
Obtrude — namucae
Redirect — reverse in space
Restrain — keep in limit
Retrieve — the gain back
sparse — not much
trace — not many

What a suspicious mind people have
Your imagination left out the excitement and climax of the evening
Saturate your mind with proverbs
Above all, don't allow yourself to be deprest by dark thoughts They become your own worst enemies

Summer 1941 It was getting extremely crowded in the ghetto. A lot of people were brought from other parts of the country and upstate Warsaw. A lot of homeless and sick people on the Street. The typhus epidemic broke out and spread very fast. People died, and often were not buried. In the morning corpses covered with paper were lying on the street. This scenario was so deeply engraved in my memory, that I could never erase it.

My mother got sick. We couldn't get the medicine. I was the only one who could past for a Polish girl on the Aryan streets. I smuggled myself out and into the ghetto. I got the medicine, saved my mother's life. It was too late for my mother's sister, and for my father's brother. Both died from Typhus.

To my very dear grandson Louis!

I feel very blessed to be today with you, and proudly congratulate you on your college graduation.

Your hard work during those four years of study brought you closer to achieve your goal in education toward a bright meaningful future.

You are very special to me. Watching you growing up was my greatest pleasure, and I am gratified looking at you today seeing what a lovely decent young man you are.

I wish you all the happiness; health, prosperity and good luck in whatever your life brings you.

With love and pride Grandma
May 13, 2003

Dear Staff,

Thank You enormously !!!

My English is too poor to express my gratitude to all of you, who made my "Farewell" event so, overwhelming honorable, fairly memorable, and unforgettable. It will stay with me till the end of my life.

Rosie's reading Wisława Szymborska's poetry, culminated the event, and deeply touched my soul.

Thanks for the concert Tickets. My grandson will accompany me on January 18, 2004.
Special regard to Dolores for her surprising thoughtfulness.

I wish you all good luck and success.
With great regards
Helena

January 1942 I reported to work to the Jewish Committee. I was sewing and repairing clothes for children.

I enjoy eating *not I enjoy to eat*

sick — sick*ness*   gently — gentleness
foolish — foolishness   bitter — bitterness
sad — sadness   happy — happiness
ugly — ugliness   kind — kind*ness*

forward backward toward leeward

Aphasia—loss of speech

obstain — powfymae
obtain — otakzymae
(v) compel
(v) constrain
(s) constraint

a broken promise

Play on the wrong side of the law
This is the only mistake I don't feel guilty.

To loose the objectivity.

Emily Dickinson.   1830–1890

Poetry in Motion

Hope is the thing with feathers
That perches in the soul
And sings the tune without the words
And never stops at all

And sweetest – in the ( ) is heard
And soon must be the storm
That could abash the little bird
That kept so many ( )

I've heard it in the chillest land
And on the strangest sea
Yet never in extremity
It asked a crumb from me

It's hard to akt rationally by highly emotional issue
Reserve distance
The feeling is above description
It is like chasing the rainbow
I don't like to be the receptience of his anger
To the point, To the fact to the bottom line.

March and April I must tried to smuggle some food for my family. We all were starving. I succeeded twice. The third time I hardly escape shooting. The last time I was caught by an Ukrainer policeman and beaten almost to dead.

"I never told anyone this
grandfather watching on the corner
mother putting a scarf around my neck
       'Don't go.' 'I have to.'

snuck out with a group of workers:
'like Em's graduation, I didn't have the ticket'"

"I didn't survive for myself. They wanted me to."

Smithsonian. March 2004
Philipino Dead mural of POW.
From Batan Peninsula—to camp
O'Donnell   Hell is a state of mind
O'Donnell was a place.—
Suffering is for ever.— it is
beyond words or even
comprehension.
Statement to the affect
definite Thread
consumed with anger for—
Our

2) Our awareness of God starts where self-sufficiency ends. We pray for health and justice because we cannot achieve *that on our own.*

Dim outline.
Phantom
A long cord of connection

On May 1942 I left the ghetto for the last time. It was not possible to come back. Round ups and shooting was every days routine. Although I still sporadically tried to send in some food to the ghetto I seldom succeeded.

"I survived and I feel the guilt"

Dreams had the same quality of strangeness. In a dream, you reached out to touch something and it dissolved (spring recess).

Being an old lady is a wretched business
like being at a party and overstaying
your time, and then just staying
on and on and your hosts are
dying for you to leave.

Letter to my Mother

You've suspected everyone of
falsehood of ulterior motives
    Fate didn't grant you much joy
For you never know a person
unless you've known his childhood
Some sort of distant relatives
sheer obstinacy   (upon)
to the best of my reckoning
destitute

"Emotionally free."
David Viscott

Modus Vivendi

Sense of duty
No significant political
importance
Generate pressure
Maria Riva
Marlene Dietrich
Erica Young
The Devil is large
Portrait doesn't have
a center portion.
Distorted the most
inexcusible extent
Purification of the language
is silent

Israel: Country of every possible contradiction and every possible paradox

In July 1942 the deportation started, and the small ghetto where most of our family lived, was first to go. I lost my entire family after a long struggle with hunger and sickness.

Negative

inability
inaccessible
inaccurate
inaction
inadmissible
inalienable
inanimate
inappropriate
inap
inattentive
(inbred)
incapable
incessant
incivility
incomparable
incompetence
inconceivable
inconsequent
inconsiderable
inconsolable
incorrect
incontinence
indigence
indemnity
incompatible
incurable
indefensible
inexact
inexcusable

injustices
injustice
insecure
insensible
insensitive
insignificant
insincerity
insupportable
tinvariable
ineffable
inefficient
inelligible
inept
inert
inexorable
inexperience
indistinct
indivisible
inedible
inaffable
inevitable
inexpressible
inexplicable
informant
inseparable
inopportune
insincere
instability
insuperable

– It was all been swept away by a catastrophe & the passage of time
– It was at the end of my rope.
– But someone awaits something without knowing it, and suddenly the slightest sign, the slightest summons takes on an unexpected dimention.
– The hidden grace of this —
– To maintain my nights
– Experience has proved
– All the daily necessities
– Try to coax her into a happier frame of mind.
– Beyond past redemption
– To make a supreme effort.
– Being addicted destroid your capacity of choice

Pronouns
Demonstrative　　That　These
Relative　　　　　Who　Whom　Whose

historic event   this is a
historical writer   politic advice
he is a political adviser

Aphasia — loss of speech
Potencial   (Potencia)

A few month later I was caught on the street in Warsaw, and brought to a temporary camp to a former High School, and send to a labor camp in Brandenburg, Germany; under my false Aryan birth and baptized certificate, as Helena Markiewicz. Later I was taken to a German home as a domestic servant.

Referring to the fact.
In memory of.
Remembrance
– Question your judgement to the level.

I have gone away from God but not from my heritage

"You send me out. Will I see?"

Dear Hospice Friends:

I have the highest respect for all of you, for your devotion toward the dying people. Your patients come here actually with a death sentence, and you provide the best care for them in a dignified way to ease the pain and anxiety at the end of their life.

I can say that I learned here more than a few operations on the computer database. I learned compassion and understanding the needs of people at the last stage in their life. I learned that it is someone here who has the ability to bring comfort at the most critical moments in a person's life, as well as help to sustain the human dignity till the very end.

I am infinitely grateful to Marion for her help, support and understanding.
It has been a meaningful experience for me, and I feel privileged that I could in that minimal scale contribute something to your humanitarian mission.

Thank you for that.

– Trust—but verify the facts   – ease your fate to the wind
                                                 – Alert to the hint of drama
– Luck directed you to desire
– Human life span—

– Monumental challenge with a spasm of rationality.

Intricate knowledge

– Your sorrow at this juncture does not concern me

– Only saints continue to love where no love is schemed

– Experience a sense of loss a sadness without definition.

                 – A brief smatter of conversation
– Renewed will to study.
– Friendship riped to a point.

Inanimate objects can't complain
– The hidden space of this.
– It is beauty it has an appeal.

                         – His Highness the President of the US
                         and Protector of their Liberties.

– To the full extend

– False sense of real being
– The condition of acceptance

Maintain the semblance of a normal life

Date 18 line. down.
 4 lines
Insite Address
 double spaced
Salutation
 ds
 Body
 ds
  Paragraph
  ds
   Sincerely Yours
    4 lines
    Name
    ds
   mw : yk

You either play your role or leave the cast. I never had the courage to leave the cast.

"Your father leaving Poland was a mistake on my side."

"This is what I didn't write about because I didn't want to be a hero."

coarse, heavy black bread and a pint of milk:
"If I only had this in my life, I'd be happy"

(Richmondtown, Staten Island, 1988:

    "I didn't say anything at the time, but
    if someone would tell me in 1942 that
    I would be here and feed the ducks
    with the bread, I wouldn't believe it."

- Steadfastly refuse to accept
- It was reluctant to admit his failure
emotional capacity
- Motivated by love
- Compress and leave behind
- A token link with supreme effort.

– Principal of unity—discrete rectified intensity.
– Someone awaits something without knowing it and suddenly the slightest sign, the slightest summons takes an unexpected dimention.
– The hidden grace of this—
– To maintain my rights
– Expedience has proved
– All the daily necessities

"I never think about them"

"sometimes I lie in bed and think about my mother—she wasn't a bad woman"

The memory of a sealed well
filled with water and leaking nothing

Therapy

: Context

Like many writers I admire, I am a writer who doesn't like to write all that much. Or, if I do like to write — which, at bottom, I do — I like to do so in a way that makes writing feel as little like writing as possible. Call it effortlessness, grace, the zone — Call it contrivance, evasion, laziness — Call it what you want: when I began this project, constraint enabled me to trick myself into being productive, into writing instead of obsessively playing poker. It's hard, thankfully, to remember now, but there was a time when poker so satisfied an urge for sameness and repetition — for choice, bracketed — that without some clever diversion from this diversion, I could have happily continued with it, depressed, forever.

: What was I trying to do?

More than ending the project where it began by revisiting concerns over artistic anxiety and productiveness, more, even, than trying to fulfill my fantasy of working by not-working, what I was trying to do in this chapter is what I've always tried to do in therapy, that is, articulate what I didn't know I knew about a well-known set of personal concerns, and, in so doing, surpass them, make them no longer my own.

Therapy

The highest criticism really is the record of one's own soul ... It is the only civilized form of autobiography.
— Oscar Wilde, "The Critic as Artist"

: Week One
March 3 2011

LOUIS: when I began this project three or four years ago   one thing that interested me about constraint was that it could be used to lessen anxieties about artistic production   so for example   I do like when people read what I write   but when I picture other people reading something I've written   I often feel a sense of embarrassment or even almost revulsion at the fact of having written   of having put something scrutable in the world

THERAPIST: well you know   you did just send me something the two chapters about your father   which I read   so that's what I'm thinking as I hear you tell me that   though I don't know whether you had that in mind when you were saying that

L: I actually didn't   though in that piece about my father   in the context of what we're doing here in therapy   the connections are really obvious   and one theme running throughout those pieces is my father's shyness   and then also my own   which is perhaps somewhat less obvious   there were definitely points in my life when almost nobody I knew   least of all myself   would have described me as shy   and this felt in some way related to my feelings about embarrassment about writing   I almost too   this is strange   but I almost feel embarrassed not always specifically at what I've written but at the fact that I'm a writer

T: well what about it embarrasses you

L: I think I'm having such difficulty answering that question   because I guess I don't know what it means to me to be a writer exactly   I like the definition   I forget whose it is   that a writer is a person who finds writing difficult to do   which is part of the reason why I like doing these kinds of recorded writing   because it's almost like writing without actually doing the work   it just sort of happens al-

most effortlessly   or as a matter of course   I like that way of working   it's almost like it almost defies some law of physics   that you have to give energy to get energy

T: right   it's a way around it somehow

L: exactly   I'm just doing what I'd normally be doing anyway having a therapy session   but it will magically produce writing that's of some use   as far as being a writer goes   it's partially that it's kind of a silly thing to do   to dedicate one's life to it   you have to go so far in a certain direction   and maybe in my own situation given my own interests and practices   it feels ridiculous too because it's not commercially viable

T: so you're engaged in doing something that may not have any tangible success

L: um in certain respects   I certainly don't rule out the possibility of success in terms that I would consider quite satisfying   but those would necessarily be in limited   not commercial   ways   I don't know if I mentioned this to you   but my dad found something I'd written in an issue of a literary journal that was for sale on Amazon   I mean a really small little poem-like thing   and so I'm listed as an author on Amazon for this one thing   and my parents were over the moon for this   and Shari and I joked that my parents probably bought every available copy of that issue   but to me and this is the way I genuinely felt about it   it really didn't make any difference to me that it was available on Amazon   but you know I think I had written in that essay on my father that unobtrusiveness was his default way of being   and also mine   and I was thinking that I almost feel like I want my writing to be that way also which is ironic because this whole project is one large performance and I was also interested   as I've gone on with this project   I've become much less interested in the topic of constraint   and in um using constraints in a way that would be by-the-book or doctrinaire Oulipian   instead I've strayed and sort of done whatever interested me   what I've mostly done in this project is given myself permission to work in ways that I find exciting and suggestive   and whether or not it's constrained   in other words   I've gotten   particularly over the last year or so   very lax about all of this   about trying to say something about the subject of constraint   lax about what constraints I use in my own writing   um so I feel like I've arrived at a place where I've given myself certain permissions   that I almost had to contrive the constraints to grant myself them

T: well when I read the questionnaire   your questions and your father's answers to them   I was thinking a lot about what the premise of the book is supposed to be as you had explained it to me   and how that resonated in reading the questions and his answers

L: yeah   at some point in those questions   I ask him what the nature of our relationship is   and he leaves it blank   and tonally there are a few blanks he leaves that are pitch perfect

T: I thought that was really so   a lot of that questionnaire seemed so poignant to me   there was so much there that wasn't stated that was implied in terms of your feeling about him and the constraints of your relationship

L: that piece is like an advertisement for why poets are always so hopped up on silences blanks and caesuras   it's filled with them

T: but your questions   it seemed to me   had a lot of unspoken communication in them too   because you know you must have been sure that he wouldn't or couldn't answer some of the questions that you were asking him

L: when I was re-reading it after sending it to you it occurred to me that if you wanted to do a crude psychoanalytic reading of those questions and what they might indicate about our relationship   it seemed like it would be very easy to do

T: well what's your conclusion

L: oh well   you know I wrote that one question   do you consider yourself a riddle   and I don't consider him a riddle exactly   but there are parts of his inner life that seem mysterious to me because he is reluctant to   or won't   or can't   articulate them   to me the interesting question is   particularly in terms of how I feel about writing   so I obviously have certain traits and characteristics in common with my father   but in other ways we're obviously very different   and I don't know   you know   this is weird   I almost feel   as I'm thinking about it now   that in my writing   I'm somehow close   like all that stuff we said earlier about silences   that that's very close to a way of being that's similar to my father's   I've never really thought of this before   but it seems interesting and possibly helpful   the point being that those questions   I mean maybe I'm just being evasive or wanting to be silent about my relationship with my father   but for me I think about those questions in relation to what it means to be a writer   well you know here's an easier way of putting it   for me   and I'm pretty clear about this as vague as I am about what it means to be a writer   I am pretty clear that it's important to me as a way of being in the world   almost   I wouldn't have said this ten years ago certainly   but that almost at this point feels necessary to me   which feels weird to say because I've always envied writers who say that the actual act of writing is necessary to them   and I've never quite understood that because sitting down and doing it is pure pleasure only infrequently   but the part that feels necessary to me is the part that precedes or goes after the sitting down   it gives a purpose to the way in which you structure your life   to the way in which you think about and do things

T: I keep going back to   I mean the part that interests me   because you sent me these chapters about your father   there must be some sort of reason why these are the chapters you wanted me to read   there are all these echoes about the whole topic of constraint   and how that's what your dissertation is kind of about   and how that's what your father is about in large part   and it's also something that your relationship with him is about

L: one question that was also blank but that I wanted him to answer   is the one where I said discuss the relationship between masculinity and constraint   which seems a really hard thing to do

T: yeah I was wondering about that   I was wondering what you had in mind

L: what I had in mind was   geez this would be really important to answer   for myself   because I'm really interested in what that relationship might be   but I genuinely don't know   it's like when you pose a question when you're teaching and you legitimately don't know the answer to it   those to me are the interesting questions but it's such an intimidatingly broad question   I feel like I'd have to then say   what are my assumptions about how masculinity works   I mean you know I guess one such assumption that seems obvious to me in this context is that men are supposed to be silent and stoic and strong   I don't know   that doesn't seem too interesting to articulate   but it felt like a question that I didn't know how to answer but would like to   and actually   this seems very relevant to my father he was not big on   which I don't actually mind   but it seems important and determinative in certain ways   he was not big on passing down fatherly advice   I remember   I've never had thick facial hair   and it didn't come in much at all until late in puberty   and I was fifteen or so and we were on vacation   and I had at that point like one or two little sprouts of facial hair on my chin   and because we were on vacation I decided to let it grow to see how long it would get   and so he saw this lone hair   I think I was coming out of the bathroom   and of course it looked stupid to have this one little sprout growing   though because I couldn't grow any others   I was secretly proud that at least one could grow long   but so   he looked at me   kind of in passing almost   and he said   "you need to shave your goat"

    T: your goat

    L: he meant goatee   but one   I mean it was funny because of the malapropism   which he does in other contexts too   my family and I find it funny   in a loving way   though he doesn't because he's a little sensitive   like one time he was describing a restaurant that was really profitable and he said   "oh yeah it's a real coal mine"

    T: heh heh   right   those are fascinating

    L: yeah so that was funny that he called it a goat   but really the point of the anecdote was that that comment was the extent of anything I was taught about shaving from him

: **Week Two**
March 10 2011

L: one thing I've been thinking about that feels important was something I said the first time I did therapy   I said something to the effect that I felt like writing was in some way a renunciation of living and Dr. S fairly strongly disagreed and said she actually thought poker was   at least how I sometimes played   and of course she was more or less correct   but I guess what I was curious about was not so much is or isn't writing such a renunciation   but why it was I felt this way in the past and still do in some sense   though less so now I think

    T: well can you say more what you mean by that statement   that writing is a renunciation of living

    L: sort of that   instead of going out and actively participating in the world   you're reflecting on what happens in it   so you're sort of absenting yourself from living so that you can document or reflect on it or whatever   I mean you're not actually absenting yourself   but to me   I guess the way to say it would be that it always felt like a necessary condition for me in order to be able to do the work

T: well do you feel like that's what you do   like that's the way you engage with writing   cause it doesn't have to be that way   it certainly could be that way   but people have all kinds of way that they write   and all kinds of ways that they live

L: you know I almost feel like uh that it's sort of close to how I live in general   I don't usually like to be bothered with lots of things that go on in the world   and actually that's why annoyingly   I've started playing poker again in this last week which is fine   but this isn't the time   I have a lot of other work to do right now

T: what's your thought about why you went back to it now

L: my thought is that I seem to like doing these behaviors or gestures that are very obvious in   relation to what's come up in a therapeutic context   so I'm talking about writing now   and in the past poker was a big thing for me in terms of how it was interfering with writing and my work   and I do more or less agree with what Dr. S said   that for me poker works along those lines   because oftentimes I'll play when I'm vaguely bothered or anxious about issues about a career as a writer   stuff like that

T: so it's an escape from the anxiety you feel about those things

L: sure   and last week I said that I like transcription because you can go on auto-pilot while you transcribe   poker is somewhat similar for me   another thing I told Dr. S is that some people who take poker seriously or play it professionally view it as an intellectual challenge   and it is in a certain sense   but it's a completely facile one   most games are   they're engrossing and involve a bit of logic but they're extremely simplistic   even the complicated ones like poker   and for me I always liked poker   and games in general more for the repetitiveness of it   and less for the intellectual challenge

T: so I mean you're having these questions about whether certain things that you do provide you with an escape from

L: from what

T: well that's the question   from what   so you know poker is an escape from certain anxieties about writing   you're wondering if writing is an escape from being more fully engaged in life in some way

L: well poker for me is an escape in the way you described   but I feel fairly clear that I don't view writing as an escape from life   it's more that it allows me to live in a way that over time has become more and more amenable to me   so escapism   which is a term I don't really like   it implies that I should be doing something else   if I were using writing as an escape from life it would imply that I should be living some other way   and I don't think that's the case   I mean there was   as I outlined earlier   a gradual unconscious rejection of certain ways of being on my part that coincided with writing   but it was less an escape than a rejection

T: well but I thought that when you said you view writing as a renunciation   maybe this is just kind of a semantic point   but renunciation is a pretty strong word   so to me it sounds like the question in there is   are you using writing to not participate in life in some way   I don't agree or disagree that writing entails that but I'm curious what brings that to mind

L: yeah that's what I'm interested in also   let me saying something somewhat different but that felt related as you were talking   one thing that's always bothered me about my relationship to writing is that lots of writers talk about the importance of community to them and when I first got into reading and writing   I was really nervous around other intellectuals writers and artists in a way I never had been around other people   I never before had any strong feelings of social discomfort   but it felt so foreign to what I'd grown up knowing   and of course something about intellectual activities interested me and made me want to pursue them further   but for me the key thing is that it was much less about socialization than it was about the work itself   so all those kinds of poetry cliques   and gossip and stuff   that feeds a big part of it   and has to do with reputations and opportunities and things like that   that usually feels tedious and uninteresting to me   I mean don't get me wrong I like good gossip   but in doses   not continually   constant gossip feels like high school   and in high school   as I've told you   I mean I had some of the regular discontents and anxieties   but for the most part I was happy   I had a couple of close groups of friends I was friendly with a lot of other cliques   played sports   drank went to parties   dated and hooked up with girls and so forth   it was all quite normal   almost strangely so for someone who would go on to want to become a writer   and as I was saying earlier today at a certain point in college I sort of rejected that way of being   consciously or unconsciously   and then you know   at least from afar some of those artistic-intellectual worlds seem not too dissimilar to me   so writers   communities   what was the point

T: I think you're circling around the question of how is writing a renunciation of life   and then you got to talking about you feel like you like to avoid the writing community   you're talking about ways that you kind of feel more comfortable keeping yourself apart

L: yeah one thing I've noticed is that I really like one-to-one models of friendship   I mean it's weird because as you were just talking I was thinking   well geez you know it's true that I prefer to remain a little apart   but at the same time I've found all sorts of ways to draw other people   friends   acquaintances   even family into the orbit of my dissertation   collaboratively   and at times I feel almost embarrassed that I've done so

T: I think that maybe there's some way that we could think about what it means to be a part of things and what it means to not be part of things   and what your dilemma is about that

L: it's like Whitman   where he says he's "both in and out of the game and watching and wondering at it"   but you know as early as middle school   I remember having pretty strong feelings that I didn't like being a visible part of a community   where you would be accountable and judged by other people for things that   for whatever reasons   I didn't really want to be   I always sort of shied away from that   right like the people who were sort of respectable upstanding citizens in the community always seemed a little too paternalistic   to me that feeling of being visible would make one subject to moralistic scrutiny   and I'm also not sure that the process of community formation   how they do what they do and hang together   I'm not sure it's so simple   I feel like people like to use the term a lot   when the process of community formation   and what makes a community continue and remain vital   is very confusing and complicated   to me at least   I mean   it occurs to me that in a one-to-one model of friendship there are a lot fewer variables at play than in a group or communal social context   which again   for me both poker and constraint are thought processes that winnow down variables to a manageable size

: Week Three
March 17 2011

L: the first thing I wanted to say picks up from where we left off last time   where we were talking about   well a few of your comments pointed out how the tension for me was that I keep wanting to remain apart from the fray   but at the same time be in it in some way   and one thing I was thinking of in relation to being part of the fray   but didn't have time to discuss   was that I feel like   and I don't think Facebook is the thing that's enabled this   but it's made it more pronounced   but I feel like there's a way in which to young people growing up   and I feel like I was acculturated to believe this growing up   not from my family   but from watching MTV   *The Real World*   watching movies   talking to friends   things like that   but the idea that seems prevalent nowadays is that the greatest possible affirmation of one's existence consists in being witnessed .   now I don't think this is actually the case   but I think it's what various aspects of our culture inculcate in young people   so things like Facebook and Twitter   which are all about witnessing others   and broadcasting the particulars of your own life   to all categories of acquaintance   it's almost like a willing submission to a surveillance state   or   even more   that one can only achieve singularity of being through being surveilled   and of course my own methodology in these therapy sessions   both participates in and reflects upon these structures   and I know that growing up I really bought into these ideas   I remember at a certain age thinking that it would be really really cool   like really super-cool   to be on *The Real World*   I can recall saying to a girlfriend at the time "you know   they should make a movie about my life   it would be so interesting"   and she at least had the good sense to mock me   but I feel like my generation   I was born in '81 and I started college in '99   which was the heyday of Napster   I feel like plus or minus a few years of that is in a really unique generational position   we're old enough to have known a way of life that pre-dates the total or near-total digitization we have now   but we're young enough to still have done some growing up during that digitization and to have for the most part embraced it wholesale   and I think it encourages you to flatter yourself that broadcasting yourself is inherently glamorous   I mean   the one major thought I had this week   was that I felt like using constraints in my dissertation was almost a way of acknowledging my own fundamentally passive nature   that in other words   I don't want to be witnessed   you know I'd rather if there were only two options   I mean everyone of course goes back and forth between them and there are probably others as well but if there were *only two*   I'd rather be the one doing the witnessing and the watching   but the breakthrough to me wasn't so much about the witnessing   but the passivity   that it was a viable way of existing in the world

T: so what I'm not sure of so far from the way you're describing it is   what's your own feeling about what you're describing as your passivity   are you comfortable with it   do you feel there's something you need to change about it

L: I think that's a good question because I've sort of considered it and I think the way I feel about it is I actually like it   I feel like it works for me   for the most part it makes me feel good   it's not like I think   "well I am sort of passive by nature   but if only I could be assertive or dominant or aggressive   in whatever context then my life would be so much better"   in other words   that passivity is probably partially temperamental   but I feel like it's also partially a decision   a conscious choice to not be involved in certain ways   which feels related to constraint to me

T: so you can use it as an avoidance sometimes

L: no you know   last week I was very reluctant to describe writing as an avoidance   it was a diagnosis I didn't necessarily agree with and similarly here   when you were saying   do you be passive as an avoidance   I mean certainly it has to contribute on some level but I for some reason would insist that it's a choice that carries certain values with it   in other words   it's not just   oh I'm not aggressive because I'm really afraid x y or z will happen   rejection or whatever doesn't worry me   it's more that the traditional or conventional subject position   that I'm setting up as my straw man here   the position of the alpha male   or the Casanova   is a position that   you know   it's not just that I want to be passive because that's how I am   it's that there's something a little problematic or distasteful about certain other ways of being   and actually   that feels very much related to the desire to remain above the fray that I articulated last week   I mean I can recall telling a friend several years ago   and at the time it felt like a big revelation to me   I remember saying to him that I felt like there was no way of being in the world that wasn't fundamentally absurd in some way   and I was thinking also this week   about ideas of being above the fray   and one thing I haven't said is that   this is actually   it's hard to know how much of it   especially at this point   I've picked up from Shari   but she is someone who very much carries herself as being above the fray   which I sort of like   I did and do find it attractive in various ways   but it's also isolating   you know for her it works   as best as I can tell   but what was interesting to me is not that Shari is or isn't a certain way   but I know very clearly from being on intimate terms with her that   heh heh   it comes with a pretty strong sense of superiority   that being above the fray is never just   about not wanting to participate   I mean I don't particularly care about vague personal feelings of superiority   I'm not deeply invested in them   like for example you could say that my decision to write an un-academic academic book is a way of trying to remain outside the fray of academic discourse   and there absolutely is a sense in which   and I'm reluctant to admit it   and this will probably be the only place in the book where I will   but there is a sense in which I consider what I'm doing better or more interesting than academic scholarship   otherwise why take the pains of doing it this way   so there is that   but   at the same time   ultimately   I really don't care which is better or worse   neither is   they're just different things   and that kind of hierarchical better-worse sort of thing is actually irrelevant   so I think those dynamics are in play   and the other interesting thing I thought this week is that   unlike Shari   my father   who's definitely someone outside the fray   nonetheless doesn't consider himself above the fray either   that's not a common distinction   I'm really parsing hairs here   but I think it's a useful distinction in relation to the stuff we've talked about in past weeks about my father   he's just an outsider by nature   but it doesn't   insofar as I can tell   it doesn't stem from feeling better or different or worse or rejecting people   it's just temperamentally how he operates   how are we doing on time

    T: there's about five minutes

    L: the one other major   let me read this thought I jotted down during the week   because there's no context for it in terms of our session so far   I wrote that   "to write   you can't not expose yourself   put yourself on the line   and stake something meaningful"   and I can't remember in what context   oh you know why because I've been revising the whole project this past week   and what I realized is   some of my new revisions   and some of the introductory materials I already had   are framing the project in gambling terms   as a kind of wager or gamble   I've realized that taking chances underlies so much of this project   underlies how I imagine intellectual discovery happens   taking chances   weighing risks   I've basically been using constraint as a way to take calculated risks   it sort of to me almost accounts for why   from the first time I ever published something   I included   almost as a throwaway   a line in my bio about how I'm a part-time professional poker player   which is factually correct   I make more money from poker than I do from teaching   but it's a little off-color to include that in my bio   is it necessary   and it's not necessary strictly speaking   but there must be some part of me that imagines that it is   in terms of how I imagine myself not just as a person but as a writer   um and you know   I don't know   that seemed really suggestive to me in relation to passivity and not wanting to be visible   that when you write you can't not put something on the line   and I think the something that's being put on the line the thing that's being wagered   is yourself   you know I've always sort of felt that way   and I've always sort of felt   and I think this relates to what I consider my fundamentally retiring nature   I've always sort of felt that that's the real difficulty of writing as a vocation and that's why it feels like so much is at stake   at least to the writer him or herself

T: so do you feel like the technique of constraint   and the different ways you have   of recording what you're saying and transcribing it   all these ways that you've described as passive forms of getting writing done   do you see them all as ways to try to grapple with what feels difficult with putting yourself on the line

L: they almost feel like solutions to me   given that it's the case that you can't not put yourself on the line   and given that I don't particularly like that aspect of it   but I still like doing the thing for some reason   then how can I do the thing in a way that works for me   and actually   working with constraint makes writing like doing a puzzle or playing a game   which as I've said to you   part of what I like about poker   and game playing in general   it's not just the repetitiveness   but the use of logic and the winnowing down of choices   you know maybe the last thing I'll say quickly is that Wayne had said   talking about that feeling of embarrassment or revulsion that I previously mentioned   he said he has a roughly similar feeling   and he said something to the effect that um   for him   it's just part of the process   he doesn't know how to eliminate it from the process   which makes sense to me   but that to him it's usually a sign that something interesting is happening   that if you're not having those feelings of humiliation or antipathy about what you've written   in a way   he didn't formulate it this way but it fits with what I've been saying   if you're not having those feelings then you actually aren't taking risks that are in some way meaningful enough

The Defense

: Context

The first draft of this book was written as my doctoral dissertation in English at the CUNY Graduate Center. That version contained ninety-nine chapters, in homage to the ninety-nine chapters in Raymond Queneau's *Exercises in Style*, with explanatory introductions to each chapter written by a fictional editor named Luke Giombrotto. The following chapter is a recorded and edited transcription of my dissertation defense.

: What was I trying to do?

Now that I've made significant alterations to this project—cutting its size by more than half, eliminating the fictional editor, and writing new chapter introductions, revising the chapters that didn't get cut—this Defense serves not only as recursive coda to the whole but also as archaeological record of the original version. As with all such records, the fossils ghost a knowledge that, in retrospect, seems poetic, late.

The Defense

CUNY Graduate Center
April 29 2011
4:02 p.m.

AMMIEL ALCALAY: I was telling Joan Retallack about Louis' project just now and she had a very good comment   she said that the constraints apparently didn't work in terms of length

ALL: heh heh

LOUIS BURY: yeah   that was one theme of it   among many   too many

WAYNE KOESTENBAUM: do you want to launch   shall we begin

LB: yeah

WK: we've already begun   so the way this goes   as I think you know   is that you make whatever kind of statement you want to make   of any kind   about the process   what you learned   what you like   what you don't like   where you want to go   state of the art   and then we make our comments   and then we have a conversation and we go from there

LB: sure   well first   I'm very relieved to be near the end of this and second   what I'm most excited about   in getting to do this defense   other than just making it official and completing the project   is getting to hear responses from three readers I really respect   I feel like   particularly with the character of Giombrotto   the project's fictional editor   so much of the project theorizes about itself   so what interests me the most at this point is hearing it talked about by others   and not just hearing myself talk about it

WK: you've powered   you've created   I think Bloom would have called it something   transumption   or I don't know what it is   but that you've so powerfully used to take the transcript as an art and critical tool in here   you have interpolated everything that we say already in a very powerful and scary way   and that's sort of an uncanny and not totally pleasant feeling

ALL: heh heh

LB: yeah   I wondered   not just in terms of you   but in terms of all the other people that I brought into the orbit of the project   I did have qualms at various points about   if not the ethics of it   if that sounds too grand   just how they would feel about it   it came up in relation to my immediate family when I did those chapters on my father

WK: that was almost like a joke   because I'm going to allow my colleagues to begin and take up most of the time

AA: Mary Ann   you want to

MARY ANN CAWS: I'm deeply embarrassed   I have not seen this because I got the wrong one   and so *mea culpa* a thousand times   I'm fascinated by Oulipo and all that I see here   I seem to have gotten the wrong thesis   and I don't know what to say except I'm deeply embarrassed   but never mind   that will probably fit into what you're doing

ALL: heh heh

LB: I think it will

MC: Ammiel   I noticed the last line in your copy of the project "I feel constrained by the recorder"   *me too*

ALL: heh

MC: will I ever see it in   as it were   a hard copy   I thought I got it   but I must have gotten somebody else's

LB: sure   at whatever point you'd like

MC: well I'm deeply embarrassed but that's happened to me before not like this

WK: wait   maybe I supervised the wrong project

ALL: ha ha

AA: okay   well   hmm   I don't even know where to begin   I guess I would begin with maybe a provocative question   if one of the practices of traditional scholarship has to do with authority   where are you getting your authority from

LB: I think it's a great question to start   there are a few places in the project where I theorize what I'm doing in terms of essay writing   and one of the things that theorists of the essay   who are mostly essayists themselves   so one of the things that essayists often say about their practice   is that without any sort of expertise in one particular area   essays take on a whole variety of different topics   the writer may not be authoritatively expert on a given subject   the essay then has to provide authority within itself   similar to Aristotle's notion of ethos   so without saying I've necessarily done that within my own project   that would be one provisional answer I'd want to try to offer   that I'm not prov   establishing authority   "establish" might be the better verb there   I think I do have expertise obviously   but I think that would be one possible answer   another thing that comes to mind might be   and this seems like a somewhat easier response   but there are poetic traditions   beyond just Oulipo itself   traditions of writing about or approaching subjects poetically   I think Charles Bernstein was the one who coined the term "applied poetics"   using poetic techniques outside the realm of poetry proper   which methodology would necessarily have a complicated relationship to authority

WK: can I ask a piggyback question   because how I would have answered that on your behalf is different   can you say something about your tone   the by and large not colloquial tone that you strike in this   because my immediate thought was that one way that you get authority is through a kind of   "imperial" isn't the right word   but you have a kind of syntax   and a gravity of voice   despite   there's a lot of jokes and a lot of colloquialisms but you're quite constrained within a formal and somewhat baroque way of expressing yourself that claims authority   even if it's sometimes a Nabokovian mock-authority

LB: I don't know if that's exactly by design as an authority cultivating gesture   I feel like it's almost the default way I write and I try to unsettle that or force myself out of rigidly working that way   and I do that because I almost feel like it's too serious in some ways

WK: you don't write like a guy who just got drunk in High School and played sports as you described   it's almost antiquarian   the way you write

LB: I'm probably compensating   or have been for the last decade or something

MC: and that was exactly the question I was going to ask having not read it   about voice   if you faked an authoritarian voice might that not at some point give you the authority which you didn't think you had

LB: I think the larger question of voice is a really important one to the whole project and to questions of constraint   I felt at points that I was almost trying   through writing in so many different ways to act like a ventriloquist   which is something Gilbert Sorrentino does a lot in his novels   especially *Mulligan Stew* but the one voice I don't adopt   by and large   is the voice of what I'll call   for simplicity's sake   normal scholarly prose   that way of writing always felt foreign or difficult to me

WK: let me just say one more thing and then I promise   I'm doing the worst   you cannot say you're not going to speak and then speak   which is what I'm doing   but let me just say this one thing and then I'm going to take the total vow of silence   isn't though if one took the 670 pages and found all the sentences that actually do sound like regular academic writing   you would probably have a 200-page thesis   some of which would be mock-academic writing because in fact what's strange   you actually have a very formal stately kind of academic writing style   that's the dirty secret of this dissertation   you don't write like an impressionistic druggy   you have a very formal syntax   you like pointing things out   you like doing it though in a mock-heroic way   you like making fun of it   you don't like really doing it   because you know   you do it a lot but by accident

LB: this is why I was so interested in hearing your responses   because I'm not aware   certainly not on a conscious level   that that's what I'm doing

AA: I guess maybe I need to clarify what I might mean by "authority"   to me authority has something to do with evidence and with a certain   how can I put it   an unquestionability   not an unquestionability in any authoritarian sense   but in the sense that the way you have stated something is   there's no other way to state it   and maybe the question I'm asking is   that probably in the process of this   I'm sure you yourself went in certain directions just to try it out   and so as you start to think about this as a block of work   what are you actually going to do with it   that's where I want you to find your authority   in the sense of being able to say "ok this was fun   but it's not really where I'm aiming this   it's not where it needs to go"   because there's a lot of temptation in the fun but I don't know where it goes in the sense of your larger project which I think is important and useful   in other words   if you're thinking about doing revisions on this   that would be very weird because I think the revisions would be much more ideological   or much more structural   in terms of decision-making   as far as what you think where your points are being made and how they're being juxtaposed

LB: sure   and I only exacerbate the problem in the way I work in that I acknowledge that everything I'm doing is by nature contingent   so as you were saying   "was this being said in the only way that it could be said"   the whole project is screaming "this could be other than it is   it's provisional   it's contingent it's arbitrary"

AA: I'm talking about pacing   pacing not in terms of the internal pacing of each chapter   which is generally really there   but pacing in terms of how are you making   how do things appear   things that in your own   I'm sure   mind   are of a different weight and value   how do you put them on a scale that will give them that weight   partially it happens very dramatically in that interview with your father   a lot of stuff starts to snap into place that brings the thing to a different place   but I think it's something you need to think about

LB: I felt like that last section   The "Clinamen" section   without me realizing it   was doing a lot of that kind of work   and I mean this is not a strength of the project   but I feel like for a lot of this to work you'd need a really generous reader

ALL: ha ha ha

LB: but at the same time   it's very much in keeping with a lot the work I'm writing about   a lot of these books make demands upon the reader   for me this is most apparent in Raymond Roussel   in *New Impressions of Africa*   all the footnotes   and the parentheses within parentheses within parentheses within parentheses   it's unreadable in the sense that you can't follow the grammatical thread of the sentences   I mean New Impressions is this extreme act of digression   but even something easier-seeming like Locus Solus is completely tedious to read   he describes everything in painstaking detail   it takes him twenty pages to describe a single aquarium tank   so it occurred to me through Roussel something about an aesthetic of deliberate difficulty   and I think that relates to what you described earlier as my baroque style

WK: baroque in the sense that the embrace of constraints is the embrace of screens   and the screen you arrived with   in a way was the tone of   I think if I remember from your very first essays that to you the essay was   it seemed to me   a device of a certain sobriety and formality   you seemed to find in the essay not   because it was a place to gush and let go   but because it was a place of a certain poised tone   and I think what's also profound in many ways about this dissertation is how rich the transferential issues are on a stylistic and ideological level   meaning   for example   you have a transferential relationship to tedium

ALL: heh heh

WK: what you were just describing   that's a very abstract kind of transference   so for example like you were saying   "oh this Locus Solus is really hard to read"   exactly   and that is the topic you have chosen   you've chosen that   it's fascinating and it's Perec's   I feel that you're very close to Perec in many ways

LB: yeah   in the way that Perec is very distant and austere as a writer   but somehow touching and poignant   you'd expect someone who's reserved and at arm's length not to be that way   but there was also one more thing I wanted to say in response to that question about authority   and that was   thinking about how to shape the project going forward   on the one hand   I feel like the structure I gave myself   the ninety-nine chapters   sort of makes having an accessible narrative through line almost an impossibility   there are just too many things   it's just too busy   but   the way I wanted to answer that question was   and I feel pretty clear about this and I feel like it's a direction I'd like to go in for future work   was of all the hats I tried on   of all the approaches I tried out   the ones that felt   immediately at the time I was doing them   and now afterwards   to be of the most use for potential future work and you know Oulipo is supposedly about potentiality and generating and making new things that are useful   but I think it's ironic that one of the not invalid critiques of Oulipo is that they haven't   I mean they've helped create lots and lots of quite interesting avenues of discovery and literary and artistic possibility   but a lot of the things that they've created are complete dead ends   they lead nowhere they're just idle literary games   and that is something I perhaps transfer or enact in various ways   but to finish what I was saying one type of work that excited me and felt useful in the way Ammiel was describing   were the recordings   I'd like to continue working that way

AA: one of the things that I liked the most were your notes things that didn't make it in   things that were bugging you   those were actually very revealing and very indicative of what kind of work had gone into the work   and that was nice to see   I always like that record of the process   it just was really useful   but a couple of things that I was thinking as you spoke   one larger question that you kind of address here and there but that I think needs to be more fully thought through   you did it with the sonnets and Keats and Wordsworth and a couple of other things but all literature has been a literature of constraint   pretty much and to think about that more seriously   in terms of an emperor's new clothes kind of thing in terms of some of these movements   and to think about what have these histories of constraints yielded   and not to short shrift them   in other words   not to think   "well it became the figure of this or that   or it became a sonnet"   it got to be that way somehow   somebody figured that out   "I need to write fourteen lines and I need to do it in this way"   why did that happen   why are these constraints part of literary production   what does that actually mean   I think it might actually be a way for you to think about how all this work that you've done might begin to start talking back to a history of literature that may not be looked at that way

LB: yeah   it's sort of the logical next step of so much of what I've done   it's something that Wayne and I had talked about early on in the project   you had said   "consider the sonnet   consider received poetic forms"   I feel like I was wrestling with that question not in a wide-ranging literary historical way   but more in relation to what counted as   or didn't count as   recent American constraint   which is the core focus of the project   I noticed that a lot of the writers I included   and a lot of the writers that most interested me in my reading around for this project   were not always closely associated with constraint and Oulipo   and it became apparent to me fairly early on in the project   that pretty much anything could go   in terms of what I wanted to look at   and how it might be related to what I was doing   you know it was the kind of project where   when I would describe it to people   people I know well or complete strangers   almost everybody would have a suggestion that I should look at   or something that the topic brought to mind for them   and I think that's a roundabout way of saying that what you're talking about Ammiel suggests   not a universality   but a pertinence   to fields way beyond the narrow focus of my dissertation

AA: I think there's also a way in which   you know   there's a certain arbitrariness in the choices that creates a quotient that you might want to think about   in which sometimes things stand for other things   and you might want to figure out how you can make each practice stand for itself   that's a very difficult thing to think about   but I think it would be an important thing to think about   it may just involve going back to your own process with each piece and trying to figure out what you were actually trying to do   so that one thing doesn't become a stand in for another   is that making sense

LB: I'm not sure   when you say   "each things stands for itself"   I'm not sure I

AA: in other words   the uniqueness of each piece comes out by its form and what you're approaching   but there is a problem at some point in which some of them seem to kind of stand for each other   their specificity gets a little lost   do you know what I'm saying

WK: yeah   I think I do   I'm not sure either what the   I did understand but now that I have to paraphrase I'm speechless

AA: I guess what I mean is   what did Williams say   "all sonnets say the same thing"   well do all Oulipians say the same thing   do all your essays say the same thing

WK: maybe the way I would put it   because I had a question about the conversations   even though I understand that it's a direction that counteracts solipsism   there are many reasons for wanting to proceed in that way   I found actually the monologues   the David Antin-esque monologues   just more effective as writing and as thinking than the conversations   whether it's because your ideas get muted   or formally   largely because I didn't understand why a collaboration was a constraint   so when Ammiel said that I thought   "what is the specificity of a constraint within the collaboration"   like when you and Robert looked at that artwork and then talked about it at Trestle   what's the constraint there

LB: there were nominal

WK: there were nominal constraints   and maybe if there were only one conversation then I could buy that the conversation here functions as a constraint   but that's where I heard Ammiel's question

LB: in the conversation Corey and I did we talk about conversation specifically   that it entails having your intentions redirected

AA: but okay   in the Corey one   for instance   one thing that came up   which I would have wanted the respondent   you to say "no" is where Corey says "well Jon is the Neal Cassady type" and I wanted you to say "no he isn't   Neal Cassady grew up on skid row   and stole cars as a kid" in other words that level of specificity   where the form propels itself out of a critical response   is that making more sense

LB: yeah   a lot more   which forms are more efficacious in that way   which have certain blind spots   it's interesting to me   I don't know why I'm so fascinated by the conversations   maybe just because I enjoy working with other people in a realm of endeavor where you don't get to do that too often   but it's occurring to me hearing your responses to the conversations   that   yeah   like that Neal Cassady comment isn't a perfect description of Jon   but   in the course of a conversation   it's not such an important point that you're going to dwell on it   you're just going to gloss over it   that actually   as much as I'm claiming that conversation redirects your line   there's actually a way in which it slides right past   there's less friction cause you're tempted to agree and move things along

AA: that's what I meant about the authority of scholarship   in a really hyper made up dissertation   you would footnote that conversation   and you would then have a fake scholar come in and say "well   you know   this is not"

LB: oh god   this is dizzyingly Borgesian

AA: okay that's what I'm saying   you've gone this far   maybe you need to go further   in other words   you've done this much   you've got a superstructure   you've got a framework   now you can think about where you want to go with it   and I think it could be very liberating   and actually allow you to use so much of what you know in other ways   that would be very odd and potentially unsettling   more unsettling than some of this might now be   I mean unsettling in the best sense   in a provocative sense

WK: I had a technical question   though I was clearly interested in   and moved by   what seemed to be a kind of notebook of your grandmother's   it looked like a transcription project   but that was one case where Luke's foreword did not explain   so what was the methodology of that chapter

LB: most of it   like the grammar exercises and then those lists were from her notebooks   reading notes that she would keep by her bed   things like that   that   after she passed away   I inherited   and I sort of culled through them for material that seemed interesting   it started in that I was trying to think about how to write about her   the Holocaust   trauma   and constraint   which is relevant not just to me personally but to various Oulipians   and I was having a really hard time of it   I so wanted it to be "right"   I don't know what being right would mean   but to do justice to my memory of her   to *her* memory of me   that anything I wrote myself always felt inadequate   so then I had the idea to just use her own material   which   as I started sorting through it   I noticed all these things that sounded vaguely poetic   intentionally or unintentionally   and then the timeline running throughout the poem comes from a letter she wrote to a friend in Israel

WK: but it is all found   none of it   for whatever reason it became very   and I absolutely respect poetic documents where one doesn't   but the gravity of that material   I wanted a little bit of an announcement or a framing   that made it clear to me   because I intuited that it was found   but then I didn't know   and somehow it diluted the possible gravity   and kind of success and austerity   I don't know what you felt

AA: I felt something very similar   but it still worked for me in other words   I felt a little doubt there about where is it coming from   but I felt that it was so strong in itself that it worked   and actually   what you just said is incredibly revealing because it actually   to me   opens up such another different level of questioning   I mean we've talked about it a little bit   I was thinking of my *from the warring factions*   which is totally a constrained thing but it would never be considered within this realm of constraint because it's leading very elsewhere   and actually this ending coda of the project leads you very elsewhere from a lot of the stuff you've been working through   and that's a very interesting rupture that I think should be examined and talked about   you've gone through all this stuff   and then you hit this material   which is found material and you yourself said you wanted to leave it as it was   and that's really interesting

LB: it felt like I couldn't add anything that would enhance it

AA: you've essentially arranged it   so what does that mean in terms of how people deal with materials   what makes something trivial   what makes something have weight   that's the kind of relative value I was trying to talk about

LB: yeah I see what you're saying now   how   at the level of the entire project   the process of selection and arrangement places or removes emphasis   I also think a frame for this particular chapter would be easy enough to do

WK: like three sentences   even less than that would be fine just so that I know   and I basically knew   but there were so many changes in discursive register within it   and I'm happy to give your grandmother   I'm thrilled to give your grandmother credit for all of them

ALL: ha ha

WK: but I was a little surprised   I didn't get   you know   it's a remarkable document   and I just was distracted by my own questions

LB: one other discursive register   I had done a quasi-interview not an interview   but um we sat down and talked about her experiences   and she said she had never done that with anyone and had wanted to do it with me   and she said she wanted to talk with me because I'm a writer   which is also why I felt this kind of weight so the things that are in quotes are direct quotes from that conversation

WK: I was curious   and it's not just because it was originally my suggestion   but I'm thrilled that it bore this fruit   the interview with your father

AA: I thought it was tremendous

WK: it's extraordinary   really extraordinary   it's unbelievable   and as you say in your later account   the way your questions   you say that "at least four or five of his silences are pitch perfect"   and I must say   also   I find the dialogue with the therapist to be really interesting   it's another example where there's something really quite unsentimental in your basic aesthetic   and so you're able to take that most dangerous of discursive situations and take it in an utterly un-lachrymose   un-codified direction   it has a kind of rigor that was moving and fully magnificent   it was the strongest by far of the conversations   it was in a class of its own because it was a commentary on the rest of the dissertation

LB: that final clinamen section   originally I had seen it as places for miscellanies that I was just sort of tacking on   but what I ended up putting in there   and the tenor of it   and how it was functioning in relation to all the previous stuff   ended up being way more important than I realized it was going to be   it just seemed to tie together a number of things   again that presumes you have a reader generous enough to go all the way through

AA: well it also exposes something that I always say   that all dissertations   no matter how dry and scholarly   are very personal things   the choice is personal   the trajectory is personal and you get there in the most poignant ways   that whole thing about your parents with the book   it's tremendous   "you're published"   it's great

ALL: heh heh

WK: and I also find the gambling stuff riveting and really idiosyncratic   your line   maybe your best line in the whole dissertation is when you say   "that maybe I'm the second philosopher of poker"

ALL: heh heh heh

WK: you say that "so-and-so was the first philosopher of poker I think maybe I'm the second philosopher of poker"   it's really quite something   it's also   you arrive at a very authentic kind of humor   and historicity   and poignancy   through staying as far away as possible from it

LB: yeah   that stuff about the personal nature of the project is important because I think constraint isn't considered a personal way of writing   in that Q&A at the Oulipolooza talk that's in the last section   someone asked that exact question about the evacuation of the subject in constraint and conceptual poetry   it could even apply to Language poetry   which is in the same rough lineage but it's absurd to say that these kinds of writing aren't personal which is the common party line   and Perec again   especially in something like *A Void*   is the one for me where this is obvious that it's impersonal because he can't handle how personal it is   or that's his way of dealing with personal matters

MC: can you say a word about   because you mentioned before how Oulipo in the American version has changed recently   has it changed   can you tell me how it has changed

LB: sure yeah   it was somewhat surprising to me   at least when I started researching this project   how many so-called experimental American writers   poets especially but also others claimed Oulipo as some level of influence   and while there is a lot of work in the last decade or two happening under that banner there's no American analogue   which is fine   but one of the important things about Oulipo is the supper club aspect of it   it started as this group of friends   which is part of what I really like about it   they didn't have ambitions to take over the French literary world   they just wanted to have a little bit of fun together   it's mock-serious from the start   but that clubbiness becomes something very different in an American context   where these techniques get more polemicized   and in an American context too uh the figures   North Americans who you could say have written major works in this tradition   would be like Christian Bök   Harryette Mullen   uh Doug Nufer   I mean one thing about this project is that it's so sprawling I can't even remember who the heck I've written about

MC: so do the constraints change   what interests me is also the rules   how the clubbiness or non-clubbiness works with the ruliness or non-ruliness

LB: I think that's an interesting question because a lot of the constraints that some of these writers have invented   let me make it more concrete   Doug Nufer for example wrote *Never Again* which is a 200-page novel in which no word gets repeated   no article   no verb   so there's no Oulipian who ever attempted that before but their example obviously inspired him to veer off in that direction   but you know the pyrotechnics in that book exceed in terms of magisterial literary   I mean it doesn't have to be magisterial   but just genuinely interesting or impressive literary accomplishments   a lot of the Americans do pretty useful and novel things

AA: it's an American thing   bigger and better

LB: heh heh yeah   how do you top a constraint   in terms of degree of difficulty   Never Again is about as hard as it gets   and what I wanted to say too   in response to your question   I think what you could vaguely call the politics of constraint   I think changes as the context changes   though I will admit that in my project I make that claim a few times and then never really follow up on it   but I do think that is more or less the case   at least at first glance there are a fair amount of politicized American constraint writers   one thing that stands out in this regard is that Les Figues collection   *The nOulipian Analects*   edited by Christine Wertheim and Mathias Viegener   which contains Juliana Spahr's and Stephanie Young's foulipo manifesto   where they critique the group's androcentrism   and uh these are you know not just isolated books or texts   but ideologies of constraint   that are politically motivated in a way that Oulipian constraints are often less so

AA: you may want to think about having some unfriendly voices in the mix   it was curious to me that you didn't take that tack   that you didn't have a vitriolic critic doing a hostile review

LB: the one book I had planned to do something like that with was by this playwright Mark Dunn   who wrote this constrained novel called *Ella Minnow Pea*   which is the name of the protagonist that's a pun on LMNOP   and it's this novel where there's some sort of placard on the town square under a statue of this town's founder and the placard is a pangram   a sentence in which every letter of the alphabet appears once   in the shortest space possible   and so this placard provides sort of the governing ideology of the town which is just off the eastern coast of the US   it's an independent commonwealth   so they live according this placard   but letters start falling off of it   and then as the letters fall off those letters become unavailable for use in the narrative   and it changes the laws of the society

MC: oh that's very nice

LB: well my description is as exciting as the book gets

MC: it sounds fascinating   is it deliberately uninteresting

LB: no no no   I hate to use this as a put down   but it's very middlebrow   that's more a reflection on my own tastes and values I don't know   I mean   it was bad enough that   before I ever even talked to anyone else about it   as I was reading it   I was writing angry notes in my book   it really annoyed me   like "oh this is really cheap   or saccharine   or whatever"   and I did have designs on writing something venomous   but then as I went on   I decided that I only wanted to deal with things that I like

AA: well working against your own instincts could be another form of constraint   like   here's something you love   write a vitriolic critique of it

LB: yeah your comment earlier Ammiel   suggests to me that there are all sorts of Borgesian possibilities   I've so far dipped my toe in the shallow end of the Borges pool   but I think you could take a dive in the deep end if you really wanted   though I'm not sure I want to

WK: just also I think that the pleasure for you as I imagine it will be   in the next step   in exiting the labyrinth   rather than further embroidering the labyrinth   that's not just about you but generically about projects that seem to ask for more and more layers of Borgesian complexity   and that sometimes really the exit is the door that should be opened

MC: with a big sign   "I'm leaving"

AA: "Fire"

LB: I'm at that point   I don't know where the door is   but I'm running for it

WK: I think something that Sontag quoted Barthes saying is that "the aesthetes' prerogative is to move on"

LB: yeah   I deeply feel that right now   and that was   if I didn't say this earlier in response to Ammiel's point about the final section   that was one of the most interesting aspects of putting that section together   the therapy   the familial stuff   stuff like that   they were signs to me that I had moved on   the most interesting development to me in the last year is that I couldn't give a crap about constraint

ALL: heh he

LB: I'm exaggerating   but it's what happens   I've been re-reading Geoff Dyer lately for inspiration   the one I've been re-reading is *Out of Sheer Rage*   which is a book about his failure to write a book about D. H. Lawrence   and he says that in writing his Lawrence book he won't want anything to do with Lawrence again   it's almost like purging yourself of it

AA: in terms of what Wayne said about moving on I totally agree   my point is more   you don't want to over-embroider it   but you will want to do something with this   because it's a big piece of work   and I think tracking your own exit out of it will be very telling in figuring out what to do with it

WK: because that's the entrance for the reader actually   when you see the light at the end of the tunnel   that's the light that you can shed back to show somebody that it's worth stepping into the labyrinth

LB: I think that's important to me too   because my whole methodology these past three or four years has been to just blindly walk ahead in the dark   and follow interests   and whims   and you know have some vague sense of duty in terms of topics and texts I'd like to cover   but more just see where it leads   and then see where that leads   and so if it's a labyrinth that I've been constructing I think it would behoove me to be mindful of how I'm getting out of it   because readers   I have to throw them some sort of lifeline

WK: and you were good about   and then we should probably wrap up   but that's just to say that you were very good about keeping each chapter quite tight   they rarely overstayed their welcome and that was   in terms of a reader's endurance   a very important strategy   because in the earlier versions they were sometimes too long   so um now this is what happens is that you step out of the room and we have a little discussion about procedure

LB: do you want

WK: oh no way

ALL: heh he heh

WK: no way   the tape recorder goes with you   this is one of the constraints   this is the last constraint

Bibliography

Adorno, Theodor. *Minima Moralia: Reflections on a Damaged Life.* New York: Verso, 2006.

Alcalay, Ammiel. *from the warring factions.* Los Angeles: Beyond Baroque, 2002.

———. *Keys to the Garden.* San Francisco: City Lights, 2001.

———. *Lost and Found: The CUNY Poetics Document Initiative, Series I.* New York: Lost and Found, 2011.

———. *Memories of Our Future.* San Francisco: City Lights, 2001.

Allen, Donald, ed. *The New American Poetry.* Los Angeles: U. of California, 1999.

Baraka, Amiri. *Blues People.* New York: Harper Collins, 1999.

Barthes, Roland. *The Pleasure of the Text.* Trans. Richard Miller. New York: FSG, 1975.

Bellamy, Dodie. *Cunt-ups.* New York: Tender Buttons, 2001.

Bénabou, Marcel. *Why I Have Not Written Any of My Books.* Trans. David Kornacker. Lincoln: University of Nebraska, 1998.

Bernstein, Charles. *A Poetics.* Cambridge: Harvard, 1992.

———. *Attack of the Difficult Poems.* Chicago: U. of Chicago, 2011.

Bök, Christian. *Eunoia.* Toronto: Coach House, 2001.

———. *'Pataphysics.* Chicago: Northwestern, 2001.

Brainard, Joe. *I Remember.* New York: Granary, 2001.

Brotherston, Gordon. *The Book of the Fourth World: Reading the Native Americas Through Their Literature.* New York: Cambridge, 1995.

Burroughs, William S. *The Job: Interviews with William S. Burroughs.* New York: Penguin, 1989.

de Certeau, Michel. *The Practice of Everyday Life.* Trans. Steven F. Rendall. Los Angeles: U. of California, 2002.

Concise Oxford English Dictionary. New York: Oxford, 2011.

Conrad, CA. *A Beautiful Marsupial Afternoon.* Seattle: Wave, 2012.

Crawford, Lynn. *Fortification Resort.* New York: Black Square Editions, 2005.

Derrida, Jacques. *Writing and Difference.* Trans. Alan Bass. Chicago: U. of Chicago, 1980.

Dickinson, Emily. *Selected Letters.* Cambridge, MA: Harvard, 1986.

Divine Intervention. Dir. Elia Suleiman. Perf. Elia Suleiman, Manal Khader, Denis Sandler Sapoznikov. Avatar, 2002. Film.

Douglass, Frederick. *Narrative of the Life of Frederick Douglass, an American Slave.* New York: Penguin, 1982.

Dunn, Mark. *Ella Minnow Pea.* New York: Knopf, 2002.

Dyer, Geoff. *Out of Sheer Rage: Wrestling with D. H. Lawrence.* New York: North Point, 1997.

Fish, Stanley. "Rhetoric," in *Critical Terms for Literary Study.* Ed. Frank Lentricchia. Chicago: U. of Chicago, 1995.

Fitterman, Robert. *This Window Makes Me Feel.* /ubueditions, 2004. Web. 27 July 2013.

Foucault, Michel. *The Archaeology of Knowledge.* Trans. A. M. Sheridan Smith. New York: Pantheon, 1972.

Friedlander, Benjamin. *Simulcast.* Tuscaloosa: U. of Alabama, 2004.

Goldsmith, Kenneth. *73 Poems.* Sag Harbor, NY: Permanent Press, 1994.

———. "Being Boring." *epc.buffalo.edu*. Wed. 27 July 2013.

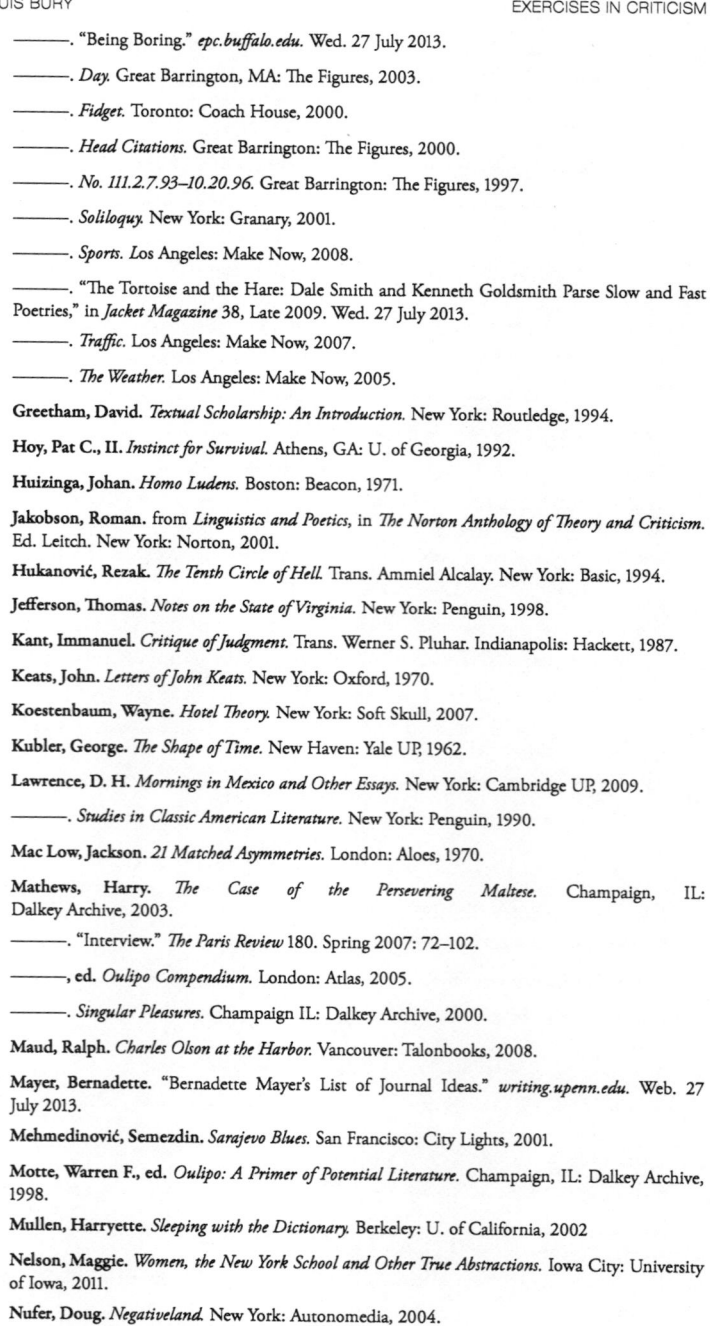

———. *Day*. Great Barrington, MA: The Figures, 2003.

———. *Fidget*. Toronto: Coach House, 2000.

———. *Head Citations*. Great Barrington: The Figures, 2000.

———. *No. 111.2.7.93–10.20.96*. Great Barrington: The Figures, 1997.

———. *Soliloquy*. New York: Granary, 2001.

———. *Sports*. Los Angeles: Make Now, 2008.

———. "The Tortoise and the Hare: Dale Smith and Kenneth Goldsmith Parse Slow and Fast Poetries," in *Jacket Magazine* 38, Late 2009. Wed. 27 July 2013.

———. *Traffic*. Los Angeles: Make Now, 2007.

———. *The Weather*. Los Angeles: Make Now, 2005.

Greetham, David. *Textual Scholarship: An Introduction*. New York: Routledge, 1994.

Hoy, Pat C., II. *Instinct for Survival*. Athens, GA: U. of Georgia, 1992.

Huizinga, Johan. *Homo Ludens*. Boston: Beacon, 1971.

Jakobson, Roman. from *Linguistics and Poetics*, in *The Norton Anthology of Theory and Criticism*. Ed. Leitch. New York: Norton, 2001.

Hukanović, Rezak. *The Tenth Circle of Hell*. Trans. Ammiel Alcalay. New York: Basic, 1994.

Jefferson, Thomas. *Notes on the State of Virginia*. New York: Penguin, 1998.

Kant, Immanuel. *Critique of Judgment*. Trans. Werner S. Pluhar. Indianapolis: Hackett, 1987.

Keats, John. *Letters of John Keats*. New York: Oxford, 1970.

Koestenbaum, Wayne. *Hotel Theory*. New York: Soft Skull, 2007.

Kubler, George. *The Shape of Time*. New Haven: Yale UP, 1962.

Lawrence, D. H. *Mornings in Mexico and Other Essays*. New York: Cambridge UP, 2009.

———. *Studies in Classic American Literature*. New York: Penguin, 1990.

Mac Low, Jackson. *21 Matched Asymmetries*. London: Aloes, 1970.

Mathews, Harry. *The Case of the Persevering Maltese*. Champaign, IL: Dalkey Archive, 2003.

———. "Interview." *The Paris Review* 180. Spring 2007: 72–102.

———, ed. *Oulipo Compendium*. London: Atlas, 2005.

———. *Singular Pleasures*. Champaign IL: Dalkey Archive, 2000.

Maud, Ralph. *Charles Olson at the Harbor*. Vancouver: Talonbooks, 2008.

Mayer, Bernadette. "Bernadette Mayer's List of Journal Ideas." *writing.upenn.edu*. Web. 27 July 2013.

Mehmedinović, Semezdin. *Sarajevo Blues*. San Francisco: City Lights, 2001.

Motte, Warren F., ed. *Oulipo: A Primer of Potential Literature*. Champaign, IL: Dalkey Archive, 1998.

Mullen, Harryette. *Sleeping with the Dictionary*. Berkeley: U. of California, 2002

Nelson, Maggie. *Women, the New York School and Other True Abstractions*. Iowa City: University of Iowa, 2011.

Nufer, Doug. *Negativeland*. New York: Autonomedia, 2004.

———. *Never Again*. New York: Avalon, 2004.

Olson, Charles. *The Maximus Poems*. Berkeley: U. of California, 1985.

The Oxford Study Bible. Ed. M. Jack Suggs. New York: Oxford UP, 1992.

BIBLIOGRAPHY

Pascal, Blaise. *Pensées.* Trans. A. J. Krailsheimer. New York: Penguin, 1995.

Perec, Georges. *Species of Spaces and Other Pieces.* Trans. John Sturrock. New York: Penguin, 1999.

———. *A Void.* Trans. Gilbert Adair. Jaffrey, NH: Godine, 2005.

Place, Vanessa. *Dies, A Sentence.* Los Angeles: Les Figues, 2005.

Ponge, Francis. *Soap.* Trans. Lane Dunlop. Palo Alto, CA: Stanford UP, 1998.

Poe, Edgar Allan. "The Murders in the Rue Morgue." *Poetry and Tales.* Ed. Patrick F. Quinn. New York: Library of America, 1984.

Popol Vuh. Trans. Dennis Tedlock. New York: Touchstone, 1996.

Pound, Ezra. *The ABC of Reading.* New York: New Directions, 1987.

Powell, Padgett. *The Interrogative Mood.* New York: Ecco, 2009.

Queneau, Raymond. "100,000,000,000,000,000 Poems." Trans. Stanley Chapman. *Oulipo Compendium.* London: Atlas, 2005.

———. *Exercises in Style.* Trans. Barbara Wright. New York: New Directions, 1981.

Retallack, Joan. *Errata 5uite.* Washington, DC: Edge Books, 1993.

———, ed. *Musicage.* Middletown, CT: Wesleyan UP, 1996.

Reynolds, David S. *Beneath the American Renaissance: The Subversive Imagination in the Age of Emerson and Melville.* Cambridge, MA: Harvard UP, 1988.

Richey, Joseph, ed. *Ed Dorn Live: Lectures, Interviews, and Outakes.* Ann Arbor: The University of Michigan, 2007.

Roussel, Raymond. *How I Wrote Certain of My Books.* Ed. Trevor Winkfield. Cambridge, MA: Exact Change, 1995.

———. *Locus Solus.* New York: Riverrun, 1993.

———. *New Impressions of Africa.* London: Atlas, 2004.

Rukeyser, Muriel. *Willard Gibbs.* New York: Doubleday, 1947.

Sanders, Ed. *Investigative Poetry.* San Francisco: City Lights, 1976.

Schuyler, James. *The Morning of the Poem.* New York: FSG, 1981.

Simpson, Christopher. *Science of Coercion: Communication Research and Psychologica Warfare, 1945–1960.* New York: Oxford, 1996.

Sorrentino, Gilbert. *Gold Fools.* Los Angeles: Green Integer, 2000.

———. *Mulligan Stew.* Champaign, IL: Dalkey Archive, 1996.

Stein, Gertrude. "Poetry and Grammar." *Gertrude Stein: Writings 1932–1946.* Ed. Catharine R. Stimpson. New York: Library of America, 1998.

Sterne, Lawrence. *Tristram Shandy.* New York: Penguin, 2003.

Seuss, Dr. *The Cat in the Hat.* New York: Random House, 1957.

———. *Green Eggs and Ham.* New York: Random House, 1960.

Tompkins, Jane P. "Criticism and Feeling." *College English* Vol. 39, No.2 (Oct. 1977), p. 169–178.

Waldrop, Rosmarie. *A Key Into the Language of America.* New York: New Directions, 1997.

Wershler-Henry, Darren. *the tapeworm foundry: andor the dangerous prevalence of imagination.* Toronto: House of Anansi, 2000.

Wertheim, Christine and Mathias Viegener, ed. *The noulipian Analects.* Los Angeles: Les Figues, 2008.

Whitman, Walt. *Leaves of Grass.* New York: Norton, 1973.

Wilde, Oscar. *The Critic as Artist.* Los Angeles: Green Integer, 1997.

Williams, William Carlos. "To Elsie." *The Collected Poems of William Carlos Williams: Volume I, 1909–1939*. Ed. A Walton Litz. New York: New Directions, 1986.

———. *In the American Grain*. New York: New Directions, 1956.

Wittgenstein, Ludwig. *Philosophical Investigations*. Trans. G. E. M. Anscombe. Boston: Wiley-Blackwell, 1991.

———. *Tractatus Logico-Philosophicus*. Trans. D. F. Pears and B. F. McGuinness. New York: Routledge, 1974.

Acknowledgments

I feel particularly indebted to the friends, family, and mentors who helped me write this book, not only for their provocations and support, but also for contributing their own words to the text, in several cases. Thanks, then, many times over, to: Wayne Koestenbaum and Ammiel Alcalay, for their feedback and encouragement but most of all for the invigorating examples of their own poetic activities; Corey Frost and Leah Souffrant, for their regular feedback and even more regular good cheer, as well as for our collaborations in an earlier version of the book; Robert Machado, for our lively conversations over coffee and our collaboration on an earlier version of the book; Lynn Crawford, for her warmhearted intelligence and the example of her own work; Doug Nufer, for his gambling advice and the example of his own work; Tayt Harlin, for our countless conversations on criticism; Rebekah Rutkoff, for her unfailingly surprising and acute correspondence; Brooks Hefner, for his eclectic erudition and for dragging me, reluctant, to Dolan's dissertation workshop; Ramsey Scott, for our correspondence on Oulipo at the project's inception; Dr. Madeline K. Lippman, for her absolute openness to the recording experiment; Wendy Walker, Tom La Farge, and the other members of the Writhing Society, for their welcoming presence; Michelle Taransky, for inviting me to participate in Oulipolooza; Jeremy M. Davies and Mikhail Iliatov, for their patience, perspicacity, and good humor in editing and typesetting the book; Wieslaw Bury, Marianne Bury, and Emily Bury, for their collaborative birthday presents to me and their love and support; Helena Goodman, for her gentle tenacity; Shari Greenspan and Ethan Bury, for their laughter, their love, their patience and support. Thanks, too, to the numerous friends and acquaintances who shared ideas, leads, and enthusiasms, as well as to the many writers and artists whose work constitutes the subject of this book, and who were all generous and genial.

Louis Bury is an Assistant Professor of English at Hostos Community College in the Bronx, New York City. He holds a PhD in English from the CUNY Graduate Center; while a student there, he played online poker on a part-time professional basis. His creative and critical work has appeared or is forthcoming in *Bookforum*, *Jacket*, *Drunken Boat*, *Aufgabe*, the *Brooklyn Rail*, *Modern Language Studies*, *Hyperallergic*, the *Believer*, and the *Volta*, among other publications.